Linking Workforce Development to Economic Development

A Casebook for Community Colleges

Edited by William J. Rothwell and Patrick E. Gerity

Foreword by John J. Sygielski

Community College Press®
a division of American Association of Community Colleges

The American Association of Community Colleges (AACC) is the primary advocacy organization for the nation's community colleges. The association represents more than 1,200 two-year, associate degree–granting institutions and more than 11 million students. AACC promotes community colleges through five strategic action areas: recognition and advocacy for community colleges; student access, learning, and success; community college leadership development; economic and workforce development; and global and intercultural education. Information about AACC and community colleges may be found at www.aacc.nche.edu.

Design: Brian Gallagher Design
Editor: Deanna D'Errico
Printer: Kirby Lithographic Company, Inc.

Community College Press
American Association of Community Colleges
One Dupont Circle, NW
Suite 410
Washington, DC 20036

Printed in the United States of America.

Library of Congress Cataloging-in-Publication Data

Linking workforce development to economic development : a casebook for community colleges / edited by William J. Rothwell and Patrick E. Gerity ; foreword by John J. Sygielski.
p. cm.
Includes index.
Summary: "Provides 28 case studies demonstrating how community colleges identify and address the continuous learning needs of their communities and how they develop individuals, help employers, and support communities as they fill the workforce training needs of the country"—Provided by publisher.
ISBN 978-0-87117-383-6
1. Community colleges—United States—Case studies. I. Rothwell, William J., 1951 II. Gerity, Patrick E.

LB2328.15.U6L56 2008
378.1'5430973—dc22
2008008300

Dedication

William J. Rothwell dedicates this book to his wife Marcelina and his daughter
Candice. They are the inspiration of his life. Patrick E. Gerity dedicates
this book to his wife Cindy and his daughters Rya, Jaissa, and Shayla.
They are the reason he strives to improve our community.

Contents

ix   FOREWORD
John J. Sygielski

xi   PREFACE AND ACKNOWLEDGMENTS

1   **Introduction to the Case Studies**
Michael J. Brna

9   PART 1 CASE STUDIES OF COMMUNITY COLLEGE TRAINING

11   **Case 1. A Unique Partnership: Lewis and Clark Community College and Olin Corporation**
Kent Scheffel

21   **Case 2. Dyersburg State Community College and the Goodyear Maintenance Technician Co-Op Program**
Bob Phillips

25   **Case 3. New Jersey Community College Consortium for Workforce and Economic Development**
Lawrence Nespoli, Edward McDonnell, and *Robert Bowman*

33   **Case 4. Novices Fill Technology Gaps**
Susan J. Wells

39   **Case 5. The CATT'S Meow**
Cecile S. Holmes

45   **Case 6. Banking Consortium Cashes in on State Funding**
Jana Bowers

49   **Case 7. Job-Readiness Program Is a Win–Win in Atlantic City**
Nancy Wong

51   **Case 8. Atlantic Cape Community College: Working Closely With the Workforce Investment Board**
Patricia A. Owens

CONTENTS

55   Case 9. WEDnetPA: The Creation of the Workforce and Economic Development Network of Pennsylvania
Patrick E. Gerity, Larry Michael, and *Tom Venditti*

61   PART 2 CASE STUDIES OF COMMUNITY COLLEGE BUSINESS CONSULTING

63   Case 10. Niagara County Community College Center Helps Small Businesses Get Rolling
Joe Iannarelli

67   Case 11. Community Colleges in the Lead With Homeland Security
Marilyn Gilroy

73   Case 12. Community College, University, and Corporate Partnership to Combat Employment Shortages
Valerie J. Palamountain

79   PART 3 CASE STUDIES OF COMMUNITY COLLEGES HELPING STUDENTS WITH CAREER DEVELOPMENT

81   Case 13. The Career Pathways Initiative at Elizabethtown Community and Technical College
Keith Bird

93   Case 14. The Career Pathways Initiative at Gateway Community and Technical College
Keith Bird

99   Case 15. The Career Pathways Initiative at Owensboro Community and Technical College
Keith Bird

107   Case 16. Brownfields Training Program Readies Environmental Workers in North Carolina
Fran Daniel

Contents

111   Case 17. Encouraging Careers in Manufacturing
Anne C. Lewis

113   Case 18. Economic Development Office Provides Career Development to Entrepreneurs in Virginia
Meghann Cotter

115   PART 4 CASE STUDIES OF COMMUNITY COLLEGES SUPPORTING COMMUNITY DEVELOPMENT

117   Case 19. Effective Community Involvement and Partnerships
Trenton Wright

127   Case 20. Building Business Partnerships
BusinessWest

131   Case 21. Housatonic Community College Brings Employees and Businesses Together
The Business Times

135   Case 22. Local Demand Should Drive Community College Efforts
Vocational Training News

137   PART 5 CASE STUDIES OF COMMUNITY COLLEGES SUPPORTING ECONOMIC DEVELOPMENT

139   Case 23. Transformation of an Organization to a Lean Enterprise: Economic Development Implications
John F. Blasdell and *John D. Piccolo*

149   Case 24. Johnson County Community College and Burlington Northern Santa Fe Railroad Form a Unique Partnership
Dan Radakovich

157   Case 25. Colorado Community Colleges: Full Partners in Economic Development
Jim L. Raughton

CONTENTS

163   Case 26. From Swords to Suppliers: The Role of a Community College in Defense Conversion
James Jacobs

171   Case 27. World-Class Training Center Helps South Carolina Companies Compete Globally
Don C. Garrison

177   Case 28. Community College of Southern Nevada Looks to Spur Economic Growth
Valerie Miller

181   AFTERWORD: LESSONS LEARNED

187   APPENDIX: ONLINE RESOURCES

191   INDEX

207   ABOUT THE CONTRIBUTORS

FOREWORD

Linking Workforce Development to Economic Development: A Casebook for Community Colleges serves at least two purposes: (1) it highlights ways in which community colleges identify and address the continuous learning needs of its communities, and (2) it demonstrates how community colleges, the people's colleges, develop individuals, help employers, support communities and continue to build and rebuild our nation. With contributions by professional educators and trainers who teach or learn in, lead, and attend community colleges, this publication adds soundly to the growing literature defining the qualitative and quantitative value of community colleges within the communities they serve.

As in their earlier publication, *Linking Training to Performance: A Guide for Workforce Development Professionals,* the editors demonstrate a thorough understanding of the mission of community colleges, the largest and most comprehensive delivery system of formal higher education to adults in our country. Throughout this new publication, the case studies provide readers the opportunity to appreciate the various functions community college personnel perform, the services they offer, and the proven results they obtain for those they serve.

Because the editors and authors of these cases are currently engaged workforce development practitioners, the reader will also come to better understand how almost 1,200 urban and rural community colleges are able to adapt to their environments to improve organizational competitiveness through training; business consulting; and career, economic, and community development activities. The editors' experience and knowledge base, as demonstrated by compiling the cases in this publication, will give policymakers a better understanding of what community colleges do, and are capable of doing, as open-access institutions serving the traditional and nontraditional educational needs of the diverse and changing communities they are located in. Specifically, this book will help business, government, and education leaders; public policymakers; and lawmakers better understand how community colleges

- Help students prepare for the workforce through basic skill preparation, transitional employment skill training, job-specific training, and internship programs.
- Help employers identify and provide current and future training programs through traditional and nontraditional delivery methods.
- Support communities through active participation and proven leadership in a variety of mutually beneficial and innovative public and private partnerships

- Build and rebuild our nation through transitioning companies into globally competitive organizations, streamlining employer services, and demonstrating economic impact from their efforts.

Workforce and economic development professionals will look at this publication as a resource guide to other professionals who have effected change in their communities by successfully addressing similar challenges as exemplified in the case studies. Above all else, this publication will begin to inform and assist lawmakers as they formulate workforce and economic development policies at the local, state, and federal levels providing community colleges the attention and resources they need to become an integrated portable training and education department within the communities they serve.

John J. "Ski" Sygielski
President, Lord Fairfax Community College

PREFACE AND ACKNOWLEDGMENTS

Community colleges are widely acknowledged to be the frontline of workforce development. Perhaps what is best known about their mission is that they provide training across a broad spectrum of programs, using many media, to serve many occupations and industries across the United States. However, perhaps less widely known is that community colleges provide other important services that affect individual people, communities, and regional and national economic development. In addition, they have the potential to do much more than they are already doing.

Linking Workforce Development to Economic Development: A Casebook for Community Colleges is a compilation of best practice examples, which illustrate what it takes for community colleges to achieve their goal of helping people acquire education and skills, helping employers, supporting communities, and building the nation. This book is written for workforce developers in community colleges and branch campus settings. College administrators, public officials, and employers also may find that this book gives them a frame of reference for directing—or judging the quality of—community college workforce developers, the functions they oversee, the results they obtain, and the services they offer. This book also can serve as a supplementary text for the many students who are preparing themselves for careers in the challenging world of workforce development in community colleges or for roles as economic development professionals.

This book was written as a supplement to *Linking Training to Performance: A Guide for Workforce Development Professionals* (published by Community College Press in 2003) to illustrate how community colleges are effectively linking workforce development to an array of services. This casebook thus dramatizes how workforce development in community colleges is expanding beyond a limited training role alone. While training remains an important role for community colleges, these colleges are also uniquely positioned in their communities to provide a broad array of outreach services—including individual career counseling, community-based economic development, community-based workforce development, and business consulting. This casebook underscores these new, emerging roles while also describing successes with more traditional workforce training. The cases were drawn, with permission, from previously published sources as well as commissioned for this volume to demonstrate the expanded roles that community colleges are increasingly playing in establishing and sustaining the social capital of the communities of which they are part. The cases are categorized into five parts, as follows:

- Part 1: Cases in which community colleges improved organizational competitiveness through training.

- Part 2: Cases in which community colleges improved organizational competitiveness through business consulting.
- Part 3: Cases in which community colleges enhanced individual employability through career development.
- Part 4: Cases in which community colleges supported community development.
- Part 5: Cases in which community colleges supported economic development.

Of course, some cases are general enough that they overlap these categories. Collectively, the cases offer several important lessons about best practices:

- Focus on key stakeholders of the community college—whether those stakeholders are individuals, employers, the community, or other groups.
- Make a decided effort to determine stakeholder needs.
- Make an effort to find out the best ways to meet those needs, whether by training or by other interventions, that will get desired results.
- Be willing to deliver programs in innovative ways.
- Capture information about the measurable results obtained.
- Communicate to the stakeholders served and other interested individuals and groups about the results obtained.

We wish to thank the American Association of Community Colleges (AACC) for sponsoring this publication and the authors of each case for their willingness to submit cases on a timely basis. Any mistakes in this book are entirely the editors' or authors' responsibility and not that of AACC.

William J. Rothwell also thanks his graduate research assistants, Tobin Lopes and Lin Gao, for their help in following up on the copyright permissions sought for this book.

INTRODUCTION TO THE CASE STUDIES

Michael J. Brna

Community college workforce development professionals and others interested in improving the ways that community colleges support personal enrichment and economic development need to know about proven best practices at community colleges that have successfully met the dual challenges in unique and innovative ways. *Linking Workforce Development to Economic Development: A Casebook for Community Colleges* has been written to meet that need, building on the earlier companion publication, *Linking Training to Performance: A Guide for Workforce Development Professionals.* Together, these publications give both seasoned and novice community college workforce development professionals a base of knowledge that will enable them to position their programs to be highly effective in their service regions.

This book is a compilation of best practices addressing the roles that community colleges play in training, business consulting, personal career enrichment, community development, and economic development. The best practice case studies presented in this book are valuable resources that address each of those areas. They are intended not only to inform workforce development professionals about successful best practices but also to stimulate thought and discussions among them so they can seek new ways to better serve individuals and communities in their service regions. The value of the book is that it addresses several community college roles rather than focusing on just one aspect of community college workforce development. It gives community college workforce development professionals several important foundations on which to build, depending on the priority for their service regions.

The table presented in this introduction provides a summary of the most important issue addressed in each case. The case studies in this book are evidence that many community colleges are fundamental to economic and community development in their service areas. They demonstrate that the very best community colleges consider the important role they have regarding economic and community development. The exemplar community colleges design and deliver education or training that aligns with community and economic development strategies in their states or regions. This alignment enables the efficient design and delivery of education and training programs that provide individuals with the knowledge, skills, and abilities that support a region's business attraction and retention strategies. Individuals who participate in aligned education or training position themselves to take advantage of the economic benefits that accrue from expanding economies. When workforce and economic development are aligned, individuals and communities grow together; the result is an increase of wealth within a region.

	Summary of Case Studies	
Case	College/Location	Summary
Part 1—Community College Training		
1	Lewis and Clark Community College, Godfrey, IL	Details the evolution of an alliance between Lewis and Clark Community College and Olin Corporation
2	Dyersburg State Community College, TN	Focuses on the Goodyear Maintenance Technician Co-op Program, established to provide training to an aging, underskilled workforce; collaboration among many parties; and development of curriculum among industry and schools at all levels
3	Various community colleges in NJ	Focuses on a community college consortium developed in response to a gubernatorial executive order making community colleges the "preferred provider" for New Jersey's customized training program
4	Northern Virginia Community College, Annandale, VA	Examines training and internships targeted for career changers and displaced workers with college degrees and professional experience but no background in computer-related fields
5	Various in SC	Describes the workforce development role that the technical college system plays in South Carolina workforce development, highlighting the Center for Accelerated Technology Training
6	Northeast Texas Community College, Mount Pleasant	Provides an example of how Northeast Texas Community College in Mount Pleasant leveraged financial resources to design and deliver training specifically for a local banking consortium
7	Atlantic Cape Community College, Atlantic City, NJ	Describes a partnership between the human resource departments at several of Atlantic City's hospitality operators and Atlantic Cape Community College to provide a job readiness course for welfare recipients

Case	College/Location	Summary
		Summary of Case Studies
Part 1—Community College Training (cont'd)		
8	Atlantic Cape Community College, Atlantic City, NJ	ACCC, working closely with the area's WIB, devised a proposal to the state to help move welfare and chronically underemployed and unemployed into the labor force.
9	Various in PA	This article addresses the creation of a very successful consortium comprised of Pennsylvania's 14 community colleges and the Pennsylvania State System of Higher Education's 14 state-owned universities. The goal was to provide Pennsylvania's new and expanding manufacturing and technology-based businesses with Pennsylvania's Department of Community and Economic Development's new Guaranteed Free Training Program.
Part 2—Community College Business Consulting		
10	Niagara County Community College, Sanborn, NY	Examines the effects of services offered at Niagara County Community College's Small Business Development Center, in Sanborn, NY, and how broad impact is achieved through collaboration with various business and development agencies in Niagara County.
11	Various	Describes how four community colleges, the American Association of Community Colleges, and the League for Innovation in the Community College are responding to homeland security challenges
12	Bucks County Community College, Newtown, and the Pennsylvania State University	The curriculum, developed by Bucks County Community College included both technical and workplace skills. The program was approved by the Pennsylvania Department of Labor and Industry as an IT registered apprenticeship. On graduation from high school, the apprentices had the opportunity to interview for permanent positions at Lockheed Martin and to continue their education at BCCC to earn an associate degree that articulated with a baccalaureate at Penn State.
Part 3—Community Colleges Helping Individuals With Career Development		
13 14 15	Various sites in KY	The Kentucky Community and Technical College System Career Pathways project is a statewide initiative that is being implemented in each of KCTCS's 16 college districts, with policy guidance and technical assistance provided by system staff in the chancellor's office. KCTCS defines a career pathway as a series of connected educational programs, with integrated work experience and support services that enable students to combine school and work and advance over time to better jobs and higher levels of education and training.

	Summary of Case Studies	
Case	College/Location	Summary
Part 3—Community Colleges Helping Individuals With Career Development (cont'd)		
16	Forsyth Technical Community College, Winston-Salem, NC	Describes a program designed to provide specialized skills to students who want a new career path in environmentally related industries and to provide a workforce with skills to meet the evolving needs in environmental management
17	Various	Outlines the National Association of Manufacturers efforts to make people aware of the opportunities available in the manufacturing sector
18	Richmond, VA	Describes how the Community College Workforce Alliance and the Center for Entrepreneurial Development designed and distributed an interactive compact disk to assist people with self-employment through small business start-up
Part 4—Community Colleges Supporting Community Development		
19	Various	Documents community involvement tools employed by Brownfields redevelopment and job training programs, including the effective use of advisory committees to broaden community representation and participation in program design and implementation
20	Springfield Technical Community College, MA	Previews attempts by Springfield Technical Community College to work with industry leaders to identify future rather than immediate worker needs as a proactive approach designed to identify industry partners and collect data important to securing future federal training funds
21	Housatonic Community College, Bridgeport, CT	Details how Housatonic Community College developed a cooperative education program to provide internships and jobs in neighboring communities for students and others
22	Various	Communicates the importance of community colleges' knowing the communities and the local labor markets they serve to ensure that the colleges are properly positioned "as a step in career pathways to fields that require 4-year degrees"

Summary of Case Studies		
Case	College/Location	Summary
Part 5—Community Colleges Supporting Economic Development		
23	Penn State DuBois and the Northwest Pennsylvania Industrial Resource Center, Erie, PA	Details the efforts of a manufacturing company important to local economy to remain highly efficient and profitable by participating in a lean manufacturing training program
24	Overland Park, KS	Details a partnership between Johnson County Community College and the Burlington Northern Santa Fe Railroad created to encourage local economic development and to provide the college with new, nontaxable revenue
25	Colorado Community College and Occupational Education System	Details legislation created to mandate that Colorado's community colleges participate fully in the state's economic development efforts and outlines the formation and role of the Colorado Community College and Occupational Education System and its partnerships within the state along with initiatives that resulted from partnerships
26	Macomb Community College, Warren, MI	Discusses how Macomb Community College worked closely with community and business leaders to shape economic development in response to the closing of the Detroit Tank Arsenal and the reuse of land after the base closing
27	Tri-County Technical College, Pendleton, SC	Discusses how Tri-County Technical College maintains close ties with economic and workforce development agencies to stay abreast of economic activity and demonstrates the value of close ties with industry to provide education and training in alignment with company expansion plans
28	Community College of Southern Nevada, Las Vegas	Describes how the Community College of Southern Nevada reengineered its Division of Workforce and Economic Development to better respond to local business needs and how the school is working to be included early in the state's business attraction and retention efforts

The key to efficient alignment between workforce and economic development professionals is collaboration, an underlying theme throughout the case studies. Among the many examples of collaborative efforts, some include only two stakeholders—employers and community colleges—but many include a multitude of stakeholders. Whether the collaborations include few or many, leadership and buy-in at the highest administrative levels are fundamental to lasting effectiveness. The more stakeholders who commit to collaboration, the better the opportunity for sustained economic growth will be. Community college presidents who actively engage themselves with the economic development community are essential to ensuring that community college programs and services align with regional economic needs.

Another underlying theme throughout the case studies is customer responsiveness. Community colleges have long been known for being responsive and flexible entities that can adapt quickly to regional needs. This is an important characteristic, because communities and economies are dynamic by nature, and a community college's capacity to respond quickly to changing and emerging employer needs is fundamental to supporting a growing economy. Being highly responsive to customer needs benefits the colleges, individuals, and region.

Collaboration and customer response are recognized as fundamental characteristics of successful institutions. A 1998 study about best practices at high-performing business and industry centers affiliated with 2-year institutions conducted by the Council for Adult and Experiential Learning on behalf of the Ohio Board of Regents resulted in a high-performance model for business and industry center (Barber, Klein-Collins, & Pacelli, 1998). It is a two-part model: Part 1 relates to service delivery, and part 2 relates to management and operations. Each part lists performance outcome categories made up of best practices; the service delivery portion of the model is designed around customer responsiveness and partnership activity between service providers and employers. The research shows that collaboration and customer responsiveness are basic to high-performance organizations. Throughout the case studies, there are many excellent examples of customer responsiveness and collaboration, and readers should pay particular attention to them.

The case studies are grouped into five parts. Readers should not focus on one particular part even though it may be their primary point of interest. For readers to understand the broad impact that community colleges have on individuals, communities, and regional and national economic development, they need to read all the case studies in each of the five parts and to take note of recurring exemplar practices in each part. Then they need to consider how each of the five parts relate to one another to better understand the characteristics and best practices that make community colleges efficient and effective supporters of workforce and economic development. This will enable readers to begin thinking in macro terms about how their community colleges are positioned to support economic development.

This book, along with its companion, *Linking Training to Performance: A Guide for Workforce Development Professionals,* provides new insights about linking training to performance at exemplar community colleges and the significant role that community colleges play in support of economic development. Workforce and economic developers, college administrators, public officials, researchers, and employers will find value in reading about how the best of the best community colleges add value to our national economy. There is the hope that readers will be highly enthused by this excellent collection of case studies and will be stimulated either to implement the best practices at their institutions or to develop their own best practices to better align their community colleges with regional and national economic growth strategies and initiatives.

References

Barber, R., Klein-Collins, B., & Pacelli, A. (1998). *Organizing for high performance in the delivery of business and industry services: A research and development report to advise Ohio's two-year campuses.* Chicago, IL: Council for Adult and Experiential Learning.

PART *1*

Case Studies of Community College Training

Perhaps the best-known role of community colleges is to provide training for individuals and employers. The case studies on that topic included in this section are as follows:

Case 1. A Unique Partnership: Lewis and Clark Community College and Olin Corporation

Case 2. Dyersburg State Community College and the Goodyear Maintenance Technician Co-Op Program

Case 3. New Jersey Community College Consortium for Workforce and Economic Development

Case 4. Novices Fill Technology Gaps

Case 5. The CATT'S Meow

Case 6. Banking Consortium Cashes in on State Funding

Case 7. Job-Readiness Program Is a Win–Win in Atlantic City

Case 8. Atlantic Cape Community College: Working Closely With the Workforce Investment Board

Case 9. WEDnetPA: The Creation of the Workforce and Economic Development Network of Pennsylvania

CASE *1*

A Unique Partnership: Lewis and Clark Community College and Olin Corporation

Kent Scheffel

Partnership is foundational to community college efforts to help businesses meet their training needs. This case study describes a successful partnership that has been of long duration.

In 1992, Lewis and Clark Community College, Godfrey, Illinois, and the Olin Corporation, Clayton, Missouri, sought to build on their relationship and established a long-term partnership that would prove beneficial to both entities. Early discussions led to the basis of what became the Olin/Lewis and Clark Education Alliance and resulted in the Olin Charitable Trust's pledging $750,000 to the Lewis and Clark Foundation's capital campaign. Olin's initial goals in the partnership were to expand training programs and to use the resources that Lewis and Clark could provide to deliver these programs while reducing training costs. Lewis and Clark's goal was to develop the resources to become a leader in providing low-cost, high-quality education and short-term training. The goal is part of Lewis and Clark's commitment to offer world-class training for Olin and other manufacturers to help ensure their competitiveness in the global market.

BUILDING A PARTNERSHIP

Various education and business partnerships were reviewed to help determine the focus and direction of the partnership, including the College Center of the Finger Lakes and Corning, Inc., in Corning, New York, and Delta College and Dow

Chemical in Midland, Michigan. Talks also focused on the culture of the company and the college and how the two entities could work together to address their strategic goals and provide benefits to each other, their employees, and the community. The discussions led to a new type of alliance based on the premise of providing better employee training and concentrating on Olin's changing needs.

The Partners

Lewis and Clark Community College is located in the Illinois suburbs of St. Louis and serves all or part of seven counties. The college opened in 1970 and purchased the campus of Monticello College. The last 19 consecutive fall and spring semesters have seen enrollment growth, with credit enrollment reaching almost 8,000 students. The confluence of the Mississippi, Missouri, and Illinois Rivers is in the Lewis and Clark district, and the college has partnered with the University of Illinois, the Illinois Natural History Survey, and the U.S. Army Corps of Engineers to develop the National Great Rivers Research and Education Center. Strategic partnerships designed to benefit students and the community also have been developed with the Missouri Botanical Garden, ConocoPhillips, and Hortica.

Olin Corporation was founded in 1892, operates 25 facilities in 12 states, and markets its products throughout the world. The Olin Corporation is a Fortune 1000 company with approximately 5,700 employees working in three divisions. The Winchester division produces ammunition for law enforcement, military operations, and sportsmen. Olin's metals division produces copper and copper alloy strip, sheet, and welded tube used primarily in the electronics, automotive, and construction industries as well as producing material for the U.S. Mint. The chlor alkali division manufactures chlorine and caustic soda, sodium hydrosulfite, hydrochloric acid, and bleach products.

Other Organizations

Lewis and Clark Community College and Olin developed the Olin/Lewis and Clark Education Alliance in 1992. During 2004, Lewis and Clark was working with the Southern Illinois University School of Engineering to develop the Southwest Illinois Advanced Manufacturing Program, which is providing rapid prototype capabilities for manufacturers and new educational opportunities for students. The college, Olin, and the Southern Illinois University School of Engineering believed that each entity could benefit by including the School of Engineering in the alliance. The addition provides Olin with a new resource when facing manufacturing challenges, which in turn exposes engineering students to actual manufacturing problems and solution development in teams of engineers and technicians.

The Larger Environment

Olin operates in a very competitive environment. Many of the products produced by its metals and chlor alkali divisions are now viewed as commodity products. The wide availability of commodity products places pressure on both the cost and pricing strategies for a company and increases the potential of foreign competition. The Winchester division focuses on ammunition for law enforcement, military operations, and sportsmen; demand and revenues have been strong in recent years.

The philosophy that guided the development of the alliance was that both parties wanted more than a traditional vendor–client relationship. The leadership of both organizations had the desire to develop an alliance that would benefit not only Olin and Lewis and Clark but also people in the surrounding community. The region is served by the traditional entities that work to enhance the workforce and offer opportunities to the underemployed and unemployed. However, the leadership of the Olin/Lewis and Clark Education Alliance sought to develop a partnership that would provide ongoing workforce training for Olin and the community, produce benefits that would enhance both institutions, and capitalize on those benefits in a way that would assist people and other businesses in the region.

Various types of workforce development training that were developed for Olin have been offered to businesses throughout the region; Olin's commitment to the college has resulted in enhanced facilities, scholarships, and services for students. Further, the alliance has worked to recognize people in the community for their achievements through programs such as the Silver Medallion Banquet. The event honors area high school seniors who are ranked academically in the top 8% of their class.

DEFINING THE PROBLEM

Olin's initial goals in the partnership were to reduce Olin's training costs and provide new sources of revenue for Lewis and Clark. Olin's ties to the campus began during the Monticello years when the Olin family donated funds for the construction of the Hatheway Cultural Center and the Ann Whitney Olin Theatre on the campus. Early discussions focused on topics such as the possibility of Lewis and Clark conducting preemployment testing to assess the math skills of potential Olin employees. These discussions led to an interest in establishing more than a vendor–client relationship in an effort to meet the training and testing needs of Olin. In a media announcement in the early stages of the alliance, Olin's vice president of administration, Don Gilkison, announced, "In the past, Olin and other companies have viewed training as an expense. However, our management now believes training to be a critical investment in our ability to be competitive in the future. This alliance will allow us to work together with the college to create the best training opportunities for our employees."

Various education and business partnerships were reviewed to help determine the focus and direction of the partnership, and extended discussions were held with the College Center of the Finger Lakes and Corning, Inc., in Corning, New

York, and Delta College and Dow Chemical in Midland, Michigan. Delta provides training to business and industry on an international level. Representatives of Olin and Lewis and Clark visited Delta's Midland Learning Center to gain a better understanding of the operation.

Training officials within Dow believed their training costs were outweighed by the benefits and sought Delta's help in lowering expenses and improving the quality of instruction offered to Dow employees. Delta responded by creating the Midland Center, which focused on Dow's needs. It was agreed that Olin and Lewis and Clark could develop a similar model, and Lewis and Clark staff members and instructors could work in the Olin Center for Excellence, the company's training facility. However, the Olin center, which is not located within the plant, would not meet the needs of the company's supervisors who prefer to have hourly workers trained near their work sites.

The obstacle in training hourly workers led to further discussions regarding the role of the partnership and whether the talks were addressing the long-term strategic goals of both organizations. Talks then began to focus on the culture of the company and the college and how the two could work together to benefit each other, their employees, and the community. The group began discussing a new type of alliance based on the premise of providing better employee training and significantly increasing the training department's focus on Olin's high-impact needs.

Problem Analysis

In mid-1994, Lewis and Clark Community College and Olin established a partnership development timeframe. The initial plan called for a subcommittee to work toward developing personal computer courses for Olin employees, with a long-term objective of offering baccalaureate courses to the public at Olin's Center for Excellence. The timeframe covered was September 1994 through December 1998.

The partnership's executive committee continued to work toward defining a master plan, and nine vision components were discussed while developing the mission of the alliance. In 1995, the committee completed its work on the partnership's mission and vision statements. The nine vision statements developed by the executive committee included detailed definitions and measurable success factors. A brief summary of the statements and success factors is shown in Table 1.1. Mission and vision statements also were completed for the alliance. The mission statement is as follows: "To create synergistic responses to the development needs of a highly skilled workforce." The vision is as follows: "Our vision is to be recognized as an exemplary model of education and business partnering."

The committee also completed its initial work toward moving the partnership to a new level, and in December 1995, it formally announced the formation of the Olin/Lewis and Clark Education Alliance. The alliance is designed to be a joint effort to provide high-quality, cost-effective education and skills training for current and future Olin employees. In announcing the alliance, Olin Vice President of Ad-

Table 1.1	Vision Statements for Developing the Mission of the Olin/Lewis and Clark Education Alliance
Vision Statement	**Success Factors**
Lewis and Clark delivers most skill-based training needed by Olin.	The amount of training done by Lewis and Clark will increase, and Olin's training expenses will be reduced.
Training must be demand driven and offered on a flexible schedule.	More courses will be offered at nontraditional times, and statistics will be compiled on Olin's impact on course enrollment.
Lewis and Clark will aid Olin in reviewing requests for training seminars.	The number of seminars offered by various vendors and their costs will be reviewed.
Lewis and Clark will serve as a broker if other entities can be found to provide better or more cost-effective training.	Records will be kept on the number of training services provided through brokering, their affordability, and the number of requests for brokering that are fulfilled versus unfulfilled.
Lewis and Clark will offer technology training to Olin.	Training representatives from Olin and Lewis and Clark will review the volume and type of technology used in training, monitor the success of the training, and develop new technology-based training programs.
Educators and trainers with industry-specific experience and adult teaching experience will be employed to staff Olin seminars and courses.	Corporate educators and trainers will be identified on the basis of their credentials, performance in the classroom, and affordability.
An individual unable to perform tasks after training will not be viewed as a training failure but as a personnel problem.	Measurable and specific definitions of quality standards will be developed, and performance measures and data tracking systems will be implemented to document outcomes.
Training will be performed at the site most advantageous to the learners.	The number of Olin employees trained at various locations in 1996 will be compared with 1995 statistics.
Olin and Lewis and Clark's computer systems will be integrated for the sharing of student information and data.	The use of technology to provide a seamless interface for administrative and instructional functions will be reviewed annually.

ministration Don Gilkison said, "This alliance will allow us to work together with the college to create the best training opportunities for our employees." Lewis and Clark President Dale Chapman said the alliance is different from any other business–education partnership. "I could not have anticipated the level of commitment and shared vision that we have achieved. This alliance has developed vision components with goals and objectives tied to each component," Chapman said.

Solutions and Resources

One of Olin's most pressing needs was for computer training, which led to the formation of the PC Institute at Lewis and Clark Community College. The institute specializes in 1- and 2-day software training. Enrollment in early courses was composed primarily of Olin employees. The variety of courses offered and the need for training throughout the community resulted in rapid growth for the institute. Today, the majority of the students are not Olin employees; they are community people working to improve their software skills. Courses are offered on the college's main campus, at Lewis and Clark's Nelson Campus, and at three community education centers. Shell Oil (now ConocoPhillips) also contracted with the institute to provide training for approximately 1,000 workers at its Wood River refinery.

While technology training was under way, Olin increased other types and forms of training for its employees in East Alton, Illinois. The alliance focused on safety, environmental, and Occupational Safety and Health Administration (OSHA) issues. Employees received instruction face-to-face as well as through videotape and computer-based training modules that were all produced by Lewis and Clark Community College. Production workers, clerical and support staff, and management have received training through the numerous courses provided by Lewis and Clark's Center for Workforce Training. After the initial steps, Olin Brass President Jim Hascall stated, "We are committed to this endeavor. It is our intent to create a strong and enduring relationship with Lewis and Clark Community College that will ultimately help not only Olin and its employees, but the entire community." The training resulted in college credit for hundreds of Olin employees. Lewis and Clark designed much of the training to include credit hours for workers interested in receiving credit, and many of the company's employees have taken advantage of the opportunity.

The safety, environmental, and OSHA training focused on the immediate and short-term needs of many of the company's employees. However, the alliance also was concerned about employee growth that would ensure the long-term success of the company. That desire led to the alliance working with Southern Illinois University (SIU) at Carbondale, which is now offering a bachelor's degree in industrial technology on the Lewis and Clark campus. Many Olin employees and community residents have enrolled in the program, helping to strengthen the company and create a more highly qualified workforce in the region. Instructors from SIU and Lewis and Clark teach the courses. After the success of the bachelor's degree program, the college developed an accelerated associate in management degree. It is now offered at Olin's Center for Excellence at the company's East Alton complex. The courses, which include classroom and Web-based instruction, are designed for adults with work experience.

In 1999, the Alliance reached a new level when Lewis and Clark's director of training and development was placed at Olin full time and began serving as the company's director of education and training. The director is responsible for training at all of Olin's Brass and Winchester locations worldwide and works to ensure that Olin receives high-quality training in a cost-effective manner. Much of the training is provided by Lewis and Clark Community College. However, the director works with in-house providers and other vendors when the capabilities of others better match the needs of the company. "What we have now is a shared vision of education to be provided by Lewis and Clark to Olin employees, both present and future," Lewis and Clark President Chapman said. As part of Olin's ongoing training, Lewis and Clark's Center for Workforce Training provided 475 courses, seminars, and workshops from 2001 through 2004 with a total enrollment of 2,250.

RESULTS AND BENEFITS

Several positive benefits for the college, Olin, and the community have resulted from the alliance. The college has continued to play a key role in the ongoing training and development of the Olin workforce. Various Olin training programs have been aligned to college standards and now provide college credit in addition to meeting the necessary company and government requirements. Several hundred Olin employees have earned college credit through the courses, thereby improving the quality of Olin's workforce and empowering workers to become eligible for advancements within Olin or other businesses in the region. Company employees and members of the community also benefit from the associate in management program offered at Olin's Center for Excellence. Olin employees and others have the opportunity to complete the degree in an accelerated format at the company's manufacturing facility without needing to drive to Lewis and Clark's campus.

Olin received a $187,000 grant from the Illinois Department of Commerce and Economic Opportunity as a result of efforts by the alliance. As mentioned earlier, Olin's director of training and development is a Lewis and Clark Community College employee, and through work with the college's director of grants, the company was successful in obtaining funding from the State of Illinois. The grant is used for Olin employee development and pays 50% of the cost of training or books. The company also turned to Lewis and Clark and the director of training and development when the firm opened a new facility in Mississippi. The director made multiple trips to Mississippi to aid the firm and developed a training plan for the employees at the new location. The director will make future trips to the site to assist new employees, determine who will provide the training, monitor and evaluate training on an ongoing basis, and work with 2- and 4-year educational institutions to establish partnerships for the company.

The success of the alliance can be seen in the number of regional and international organizations that have viewed the partnership as a benchmark for corporate–college partnerships. Organizations that have met with Olin and Lewis and Clark representatives to discuss the alliance include Metropolitan Community

College in Omaha, Nebraska; Frontier Community College and the Airtex Corporation in Fairfield, Illinois; Collegis Corporation of Orlando, Florida; Spoon River Community College in Canton, Illinois; and Shenzhen Polytechnic in Shenzhen Guangdong, China. Members of a Higher Learning Commission site visit team also praised the work of the alliance after a review of the operation. In 1999, the Illinois Community College Board recognized the success of the partnership and presented its Award for Excellence in Workforce Preparation to the alliance. The Illinois Community College Board honored the alliance for moving beyond the typical business–college relationship and cited Olin and Lewis and Clark for achieving a new standard in programs and endeavors that benefit both organizations and the community.

Olin conducts a variety of training sessions, seminars, and meetings on the Lewis and Clark campus. Workforce development classes, corporate safety meetings, employee appreciation dinners, and annual stockholder meetings have been held at the college. The company also has played a major role in the ongoing development of the campus. Lewis and Clark Community College undertook a $3 million capital campaign in 1994, with Olin taking the lead role by awarding a $750,000 challenge grant. The successful campaign resulted in Olin's gift being used to develop multimedia laboratories in the Olin Science Building, equipping a multimedia development studio, and establishing a scholarship endowment for local minority students majoring in science, technology, or business.

LESSONS LEARNED

Lessons gained from the partnering process have been numerous and ongoing. Alliance partners had to recognize and overcome employee, system, and organizational resistance to change. To succeed, the alliance partners had to learn each other's organizational cultures and how to work through obstacles with patience and empathy. A successful alliance requires total buy-in from the highest levels of the organizations. The leaders of the organizations must agree that collaborating is important and beneficial, and the leadership's support of the alliance must be ongoing and visible throughout both organizations.

As part of the buy-in, trust among the leadership is critical for success. Some areas within the alliance may underperform or not meet the high expectations of the leadership. The leaders must be able to openly discuss their concerns and address issues that could hinder the operation of the partnership. An alliance will be most successful when both parties benefit financially and work together in reaching strategic objectives. Some units within each of the alliance organizations may not want to cooperate or may want to operate independent of the alliance. This action can create positive and negative outcomes. The potential exists for entrepreneurial units to produce unexpected positive outcomes, whereas other units could create frustration or animosity within the organizations if they fail to work toward enhancing the alliance. In the Olin/Lewis and Clark Education Alliance, Olin initiated total quality management outcome-oriented assessment of teaching and learning systems, set expectations for technology and teaching, and taught the college a partnering model that has been applied to many other companies.

CASE 2

Dyersburg State Community College and the Goodyear Maintenance Technician Co-Op Program

Bob Phillips

Co-operative education programs have had a long history. This case study describes a recent, up-to-date co-op program offered to help an organization meet its training needs.

The Goodyear Maintenance Technician Co-Op Program was initiated on October 30, 2001, when Union City Plant Manager Gerald Autry and Ray Cunningham, manager of manufacturing training for North American tires, presented the concept in a formal presentation to approximately 40 government officials and business leaders. The program is a collaborative effort by the Goodyear Tire and Rubber Company, the Obion County Industrial Development Corporation (OCIDC), Dyersburg State Community College (Dyersburg State), the Tennessee Technology Center in Newbern, and the business community in Obion County and Union City, Tennessee. Because of global competition, the Goodyear plant in Union City was forced to downsize and at the same time improve production efficiencies. This situation required a change in workforce training priorities.

Goodyear identified two major problems: (1) More than 50% of the skilled maintenance employees were eligible for retirement within the next 5 years, and (2) it was impossible to find new employees in the local economy who possessed the necessary skills to assume vacant maintenance positions. Goodyear proposed that the Goodyear Maintenance Technician Co-Op Program be initiated at the Union City plant. The training program was initially developed jointly by Goodyear's corporate training staff; Great Plains Technical School in Lawton,

Oklahoma; Danville Community College in Virginia; and Kaw Area Technical School in Topeka, Kansas. This is a model program in teaching pneumatics, hydraulics, robotics, and programmable logic controllers. Goodyear asked Dyersburg State to organize a similar training program leading to an associate of applied science degree in manufacturing systems technology. Within 7 months of initiation, the project created 45 new college courses, 6 new technical certificate programs, and the associate of applied science degree based on the Goodyear model.

At the request of Goodyear and OCIDC, Dyersburg State agreed to deliver this training program to the Union City/Obion County community. The college also acted as the purchasing agent for OCIDC and in that role purchased all equipment and furniture for the new facility. Dyersburg State provided the technical support for the installation of the computer network and all computers at the facility. The college currently administers the training program, including hiring instructors, developing and modifying curriculum as needed, and awarding college credit and continuing education units to students. The cost of training is paid by Goodyear and other industries using the Union City training facility. No state funds were used for the project.

OCIDC raised approximately $1.5 million of local money to purchase and equip a training site in Union City. Between October 30, 2001, and August 19, 2002, money was raised; a training site was purchased and renovated; more than $400,000 worth of equipment was installed; 45 new college courses, 6 new certificate programs, and a new associate degree program were developed and approved by the Tennessee Board of Regents; instructors were hired; and 16 Goodyear employees were enrolled. The original 16 students were selected from a pool of 400 applicants. These employees and students scored high on several assessment instruments (including the Bennett Mechanical Aptitude Test, Work Keys, and Keytrains) that enabled the employer to determine the skills and abilities needed to do well in a manufacturing systems technology training program and as an employee for Goodyear. In December 2002, these 16 employees were awarded technical certificates in welding.

Once again because of the poor economy and sluggish sales, in January 2003, Goodyear was forced to make adjustments in the training schedule. Representatives of Dyersburg State worked with Goodyear management to revise the training curriculum, creating short-term training modules, which would be required of all industrial maintenance employees. These training modules were put in place, and the first group of employees was enrolled at the end of February 2003. From February 2003 to October 2004, more than 175 Goodyear employees received training under the revised short-term training plan.

In July 2003, a similar training program was started for employees at other industries in western Tennessee. Industries that have already participated in training at the facility in Union City or are scheduled for training include Royal Guard Vinyl, Union City *Messenger*, Vaughn Electric Company, Siegel-Robert (SR) Products, Tyson Foods, Blue Steel Tool, and Firestone. Initially, the training facility was booked through November 2004. The Maintenance Technician Co-Op Program for Obion County industries is described by the Goodyear and Tire and Rubber Company as a world-class program, suited both for current and future industrial training needs. This innovative program is enhancing economic development growth opportunities in northwest Tennessee in the face of increasing global competition.

This program is having a significant economic impact on this region. Northwest Tennessee has not enjoyed the growth opportunities experienced in other parts of the state. Despite the recent layoffs at the Goodyear Union City plant, Goodyear employs 2,700 hourly and salaried employees. The average hourly wage is $24; the annual payroll is $336,611,723. Although Goodyear is closing plants in other parts of the country and has recently been involved in difficult labor negotiations with its union, the plant in Union City has survived and continues to be the largest employer in northwest Tennessee. In addition, plants such as ERMCO, Firestone, Siegel-Roberts, Tyson Foods, Williams Sausage, Bryan Plastics, MTD Products, and Lennox are able to give their associates a competitive edge through the training that is now available at the Union City facility.

This program provides a first line of defense for retaining employees of northwest Tennessee's largest employer, as well as employees of other industries in the area. It also is a vital resource for encouraging other employers to locate in this region. The program is available for preservice training for high school students and others who want to prepare for high-paying jobs.

With Goodyear's substantial investment in high-tech equipment and technology in Union City and intense global competition, it is imperative that the plant have maintenance technicians who have the job skills to maintain this equipment and technology. Establishing this training program in Union City goes a long way toward helping to ensure that the Goodyear plant in Union City will remain a global competitor and remain in Union City. It also provides state-of-the-art opportunities for other local industries, enhances educational opportunities available in the local school systems, and serves as a strong industrial recruitment tool for Union City, Obion County, and the surrounding region.

The Goodyear Maintenance Technician Co-Op Program has been praised by Goodyear Union City management as well as corporate representatives of Goodyear. Former plant manager Gerald Autry, current plant manager Jim Davis, and Jim Price, corporate training officer, recognized Dyersburg State at the September 2002 quarterly meeting of the Tennessee Board of Regents for the outstanding job the college has done to respond to their company's training needs. Dyersburg State's training program is only one of four of its kind in the nation. Similarly, the Obion County Chamber of Commerce and other representatives of the business community in Obion County have expressed their appreciation for Dyersburg State's leadership in taking on the significant task in a short period of time for bringing a nationally recognized training model to western Tennessee.

New Jersey Community College Consortium for Workforce and Economic Development

Lawrence Nespoli, Edward McDonnell, and Robert Bowman

What is the role of community colleges in meeting statewide training needs for workforce and economic development? This case study provides the foundation for a way to answer that question.

The community college connection to workforce development is becoming more recognized nationally. However, in many states, community colleges are still not connected to the state's workforce development priorities in a meaningful way. In New Jersey, gubernatorial Executive Order #36 designated community colleges as the "preferred provider" for the state's customized training programs. To fully respond to this new partnership with the state, the colleges created a new structure to get things done as a statewide team. Specifically, New Jersey's community colleges created a new statewide "equity" consortium, believed to be the only consortium of its kind in the country for community colleges.

EQUITY CONSORTIUM PARTNERS

Community colleges are by far the largest provider of higher education in New Jersey, enrolling more than 350,000 students each year in a wide range of credit and noncredit programs. The colleges are a wonderful success story in New Jersey. However, before 2003, they were not connected directly to the state's agenda. The colleges turned to their state association, the New Jersey Council of County

Colleges, to create a workforce consortium that, for the first time, would place the statewide resources of New Jersey's community colleges squarely in support of the state's workforce development priorities. The council is unique among state associations in that it was created by statute to represent the collective interests of the state's 19 community colleges. In addition to the colleges and their state association, two organizations were key players: the New Jersey Department of Labor and Workforce Development (the department) and the New Jersey Business and Industry Association (BIA).

The department runs the state's successful customized training program through which grants are awarded to businesses to assist in training efforts. Typically, the colleges assist businesses in completing the grant application process; after the grants are awarded, businesses contract with the colleges to deliver the training. Although community colleges have always been active participants in the department's customized training program, for years, the department has encouraged the colleges to strengthen their program offerings to the business community. The department was supportive of the start-up efforts to create the new consortium. Similar support was offered by the New Jersey Commerce Commission, the New Jersey Department of Treasury, and other state agencies that participate in the state's workforce development efforts.

BIA is the largest statewide employer association in the country, with nearly 30,000 members. It too was supportive of the new consortium. It helped develop a brochure and CD-ROM describing the customized training services available at community colleges. It then mailed the brochure and CD-ROM to its members with a cover letter from its president telling business leaders to explore community colleges to meet their training needs.

WINDOW OF OPPORTUNITY

The timing was right for the creation of the new consortium. A new governor and commissioner of labor were reaching out to community colleges in new and significant ways. New legislative leaders were doing the same. In addition, the new BIA president was continuing that organization's strong advocacy for community college–customized training programs. In short, a window of opportunity opened that made new statewide community college initiatives more promising than ever.

The new consortium was a response to three related problems: (1) New Jersey's community colleges were not consistently connected to the state's workforce development agenda; (2) the colleges did not have the right business model for serving businesses with multiple sites in multiple locations throughout the state; and (3) customized training was not a priority at some of the colleges, and thus their programs were weaker than those at other colleges where customized training was a top priority.

Connecting to Workforce Development

Why were many community college systems not well connected to workforce development initiatives by state government? Why did many state leaders fail to turn to community colleges to deliver important state programs to the business community? The problem was not a lack of college programs and resources. Rather, the problem was the ability to connect state and business leaders to the right college resources at the right time. States need one point of contact with community colleges to help coordinate customized training to businesses. Further, states need a point of contact that itself has the means to deliver customized training when necessary. In New Jersey, the new consortium now serves as that one point of contact for state and business leaders.

Providing Delivery Across Multiple Sites

Many businesses have multiple sites in multiple locations throughout a state (or even in several states). By contrast, most community colleges have a local (or at most regional) service area. The result is that if these businesses want to use community colleges to train their employees, they must work with several community colleges to do so. This approach does not work for businesses with multiple sites. Further, community colleges struggle to compete with other training providers in an education marketplace that is increasingly competitive. In New Jersey, these businesses with multiple locations can now contact the new consortium to gain access to community college training programs anywhere in the state.

Providing Customized Training

It should come as no surprise that some community colleges are better at customized training than others. The same is true of all organizations (e.g., schools, hospitals, and universities) no matter what the program. Each has its strengths and weaknesses. This is the normal curve at work in the real world. One of the greatest benefits of the new consortium is that it is able to take the strengths and resources of all of New Jersey's community colleges into areas of the state where they are needed the most.

PROBLEM ANALYSIS

The reasons for creating the new consortium were compelling; the evidence supporting those reasons was clear. Feedback from the New Jersey Department of Labor was strong that community colleges needed to do something to be a bigger player in the state's customized training programs. Although the department had successfully partnered with community colleges over the years, there was a growing frustration that the colleges were not well organized to respond to regional and statewide needs of clients with facilities and employees in multiple locations throughout the state. Furthermore, department officials made clear that they would no longer refer clients to the colleges with weaker customized training programs. As a result, other training providers were becoming more active players with the state. This feedback from the department was supported by hard data from the field. Simply put, community colleges were losing market share. In the past, community colleges were providing more than half of the state's customized training programs. More recently, the colleges' share had dropped below one quarter. Something had to be done.

THE SOLUTION: A STATEWIDE CONSORTIUM

Weary of watching competitors grab a bigger share of the state's training dollars, New Jersey's community colleges took unprecedented action to create the most powerful training force in the state. The colleges created an "investment" opportunity based on a proposed business plan for delivering training to businesses and government clients. Together, the colleges put up $1.5 million in start-up capital to create a new equity consortium designed to generate millions in new training revenue for the investing colleges. To accomplish this quickly, the colleges created the consortium within their existing state association, the New Jersey Council of County Colleges, rather than creating a new and separate 501(c)(3) corporation.

The new statewide consortium has its own governance board and bylaws. Membership within the new consortium is open to all community colleges in New Jersey. Each college signed a participation agreement that outlined the legal framework for the consortium and each college's relationship to it. Three levels of membership were offered: Level A membership required at least a $100,000 equity contribution; Level B membership required an equity contribution of at least $50,000 but less than $100,000; Level C membership required an equity contribution of at least $1,000 but less than $50,000. Membership level determined participation in the consortium's governance board. Level A members received one voting member on the board for each $100,000 contribution. Level B members received an associate member on the board entitled to cast one-half vote. One member on the governance board represented the interests of all Level C members. The governance board maintains full oversight and responsibility for the consortium operations. One of the governance board's responsibilities is to annually determine the "dividends" to be distributed to the consortium members from training revenues earned. These dividends are paid to the members in direct proportion to the initial equity investments made by the colleges.

With this new business model and organizational structure in place, the consortium moved quickly to hire a new executive director and staff. The priority of the staff members was clear from the start: maximize the sale and delivery of community college training services in three ways. First, the consortium will partner with the state to contact companies identified by the New Jersey Department of Labor and the New Jersey Commerce Commission as businesses considering moving to or expanding in New Jersey. A major victory for community colleges was that high-level state agencies quickly saw the consortium as an asset for accomplishing their priorities and thus were willing, and even eager, to refer companies to the consortium. Second, the consortium will reach out to the large corporations with multiple sites throughout the state. Third, the consortium will target areas of the state in which community colleges are losing market share to other training providers.

When the consortium identifies business clients that might need training, it always invites staff members from the local college to participate in the initial meetings. In all of its communications with clients, the consortium presents itself as working in collaboration with the local college. However, the consortium is the primary point of contact for the client. It is the consortium's job to work with the client to develop the training program and write the New Jersey Department of Labor customized training application, when appropriate. The consortium then turns to the local college(s) to deliver the training. After the cost of books and instructional materials have been paid for, approximately 60% of the revenue goes to the consortium (for operating costs plus dividends paid to the investing colleges) and approximately 40% goes to the local college(s) that performed the training.

SIGNS OF SUCCESS

Although the consortium has been in business less than a year, the early signs of success are impressive. The consortium has helped community colleges reach a new level of credibility and prominence with state officials. These officials are now eager to partner with community colleges in new and significant ways. For example, state leaders have invited the executive director of the consortium to participate in monthly meetings in which representatives from various state departments convene to discuss major projects under way to serve key business clients. In short, community colleges are now at the table with the highest levels of state government as the state's economic development initiatives are being fashioned.

The consortium has helped community colleges enhance their reputation with business leaders. These leaders see the wisdom of having one point of access to the training programs offered by New Jersey's community colleges. In addition, several of these business leaders have been among the consortium's first clients. For example, the consortium, working in collaboration with state officials, was successful in recruiting a major telecommunications company to New Jersey, bringing with it several hundred new jobs to the state.

Although the consortium was established primarily to meet business training needs, state agencies have similarly concluded that they can get training for their employees through the consortium. For example, the consortium, working with the New Jersey Department of Human Services, is delivering important training to hundreds of social services aides and other support staff throughout the state.

Less than 100 days after the first meeting with Department of Human Services staff, the consortium developed a new certificate of competency in child protective services, trained 46 qualified instructors, and launched the first classes at more than a dozen sites throughout the state. The consortium has already generated enough revenue to cover all of its operating costs for the first year. The business plan anticipates annual gross revenue of approximately $3 million, with $1 million returned to the investing colleges each year.

LESSONS LEARNED

The most important lesson learned in the creation of the New Jersey Consortium for Workforce and Economic Development was that commitment to community can hurt community colleges. Commitment to community is, after all, a cornerstone of the community college mission, so it might be surprising that loyalty to community could ever be bad for community colleges. The colleges were created, first and foremost, to serve the needs of their local communities, and they continue to operate with a real passion to that end. However, when commitment to community is so strong that a college becomes parochial, that is not a good thing. Such a college will be less likely to seek partnerships with neighboring community colleges, and such a college will be less likely to see itself as part of the statewide community college team.

Applied to the new workforce consortium in New Jersey, this kind of parochialism led some colleges to initially see the consortium as "them" rather than "us." That is, some saw the consortium as a threat—another organization they would have to compete against—rather than as a new resource that would benefit all of the community colleges working as a statewide team. Special efforts were made to be sensitive to this early concern of some of the colleges. As the consortium staff began to connect with clients, two important principles contained in the consortium's bylaws were honored at all times.

First, it was agreed that the consortium would refrain from providing training to businesses that were already clients of one of the member colleges. The purpose of the consortium, after all, was to find new business. However, it is important to recognize that, as a practical matter, it is not always immediately clear that a company has a prior relationship with a college. Good communication between the consortium and campus staff is a necessity. Even more importantly, there must be trust and goodwill between the consortium and campus staff. When misunderstandings occur, the consortium will always defer to a member college's wishes with regard to a particular client.

Second, when the consortium finds new clients, it will turn first to the local community college in that area to deliver the training or to participate in a portion of the training. This action will ensure that colleges share in some of the training revenue at the beginning of a project in addition to the dividends paid at year's end. Again, trust and goodwill obviously come into play here too. Different colleges will likely take the lead on different projects, depending on the client's needs and the strengths and expertise of individual colleges, but the priority is to get the local colleges as involved as possible as quickly as possible.

These are exciting times for community colleges. The role of community colleges in workforce development is being widely promoted by key policymakers in state houses across the country. However, there are many significant challenges ahead before community colleges reach their full potential as the key workforce development partner of the states. We need new structures to meet those new challenges. The new workforce consortium in New Jersey is precisely the kind of new structure needed in our state. In addition, we believe it has great potential as a national model for community college workforce development programs.

CASE 4

Novices Fill Technology Gaps

Susan J. Wells

Community colleges play many roles in meeting training needs. This case study documents a specific program that is intended to help employers meet their unique needs for technology talent.

Inside a suburban Washington, DC, office building, 25 college graduates ranging in age from 25 to 55 are going back to school. None of them has a computer technology background, but all are sitting at personal computers from 9 a.m. to 4 p.m., 5 days a week, to learn the basics of computer programming and system networking. Many of them have quit careers to be here. Others are reentering the workforce. Still others are retirees looking for extra income.

Whatever their backgrounds, they are all counting on the same thing: They expect their newfound knowledge and skills to prepare them to join one of the hottest job markets today—information technology (IT). This 6-month crash course is the Technology Retraining Internship Program or TRIP. Northern Virginia Community College (NVCC) in Annandale, Virginia, launched TRIP in January 1998 as one solution to the insatiable demand for qualified employees in Northern Virginia's technology industry.

The program targets career changers and displaced workers who have college degrees and professional work experience but no backgrounds in computer-related fields. To move these students quickly into IT careers, TRIP seeks to leverage a student's past work experience and academic training plus something else: hands-on training through paid internships with local IT companies. The program is getting attention as a model public–private partnership, and its graduates are turning internships into jobs. "The traditional stuff just is not working anymore, so we've really had to look elsewhere and in other ways to get qualified people," said Cheryl Orr, former director of human resources at Dynamic Technology Systems, Inc., a 102-employee IT firm in Alexandria, Virginia. Students in TRIP "all have degrees and they've sacrificed to do this—quitting their previous jobs to devote full-time to their recareering. The commitment is there, and those are the kind of people we want to employ."

IT WORKERS WANTED NOW

TRIP is one of several workforce development initiatives sponsored and partially funded by the Northern Virginia Regional Partnership Inc. (NVRP), a 2-year-old coalition of educators and local technology executives. With a $2.4 million state grant earmarked for technology education and workforce development, the partnership's aim is to attract and train new workers, particularly those in nontechnological fields who want to make career transitions toward IT jobs. That mandate is crucial. Virginia needs IT employees. With an estimated 2,055 technology firms in Northern Virginia, the region's technology sector represents 70% of all technology earnings in the state. A 1998 study commissioned by the NVRP estimated that there were 22,987 vacancies among Northern Virginia's IT firms, largely in the software engineering and programming fields. Companies polled for the study also anticipated that the current need for IT customer service, management, and engineering services would double—and in some cases triple—over the next 2 years, according to the study's authors at George Mason University's Institute for Public Policy in Fairfax, Virginia.

The region's high-tech labor crunch mirrors that of the nation. The Information Technology Association of America, an 11,000-member business group based in Arlington, Virginia, conducted a survey in 1999 and found that a lack of skilled workers was the most significant barrier to growth that IT companies face. Based on the responses of 57 firms, the research indicated that companies place the worker shortage in front of national economic conditions, profit margins, or the lack of capital investment as an obstacle to expansion. California, Texas, and Virginia will have the largest numbers of IT workers in the country by 2006, predicted a report released in July 1999 by the U.S. Department of Commerce's Office of Technology Policy. Following those states in the IT employee ranks will be Oregon, Georgia, and Colorado.

A CURE FOR JOB-HOPPING?

To help meet Virginia's need for IT employees, the regional partnership and NVCC struck a deal. Annual support from NVRP partially offsets the institutional costs of TRIP, and local high-tech companies help sponsor the training by providing paid internships to students, said Pete White, TRIP's program coordinator at the community college. The program so far appears to be working. As of July 1999, 90 students had graduated from the first four sessions, and 81 had landed technology jobs with local companies at annual salaries averaging $35,400, according to White. The program's popularity is growing, he said, "I get two to three phone calls a day from parties interested in TRIP."

Roy Marshall made such a call in 1997 after retiring from a 27-year career in the U.S. Army. Although his military work had not focused on hands-on technology, Marshall, 52, always had a strong interest in the field. He entered the TRIP program in May 1998 and took an internship with Walcoff & Associates Inc., an IT company in Fairfax, Virginia. When he graduated in October, Marshall was offered a full-time position with Walcoff providing network and user support in the firm's computer center as a local area network analyst.

"You go to a job fair, and companies will say they have no entry-level positions, that they want folks with experience," Marshall said. "This program takes people who have experience and gives them a foot in the door with enough basic tech skills to give them confidence, plus some real-world time working with a company." Marshall's experience now has come full circle. He accompanied company officials on a recent visit to a TRIP class to help make a presentation to a new set of potential interns. "I wish we could hire 10 more just like him," said Rosanne Gorkowski, Walcoff's director of human resources.

Local employers say they are drawn to TRIP partly because of the high level of commitment it requires. They are expecting that to translate into better-qualified hiring prospects who do not want to job hop. "The level and caliber of people you get from TRIP is what attracted us," said Gorkowski. "These students are really making a commitment even though they may be lacking technical skills going in, they've committed time and money to learning, they're more mature and know what they need to do to be successful."

Not Your Usual Interns

TRIP's admissions process is selective. Requirements include a bachelor's degree and a demonstrated aptitude for technical study, which is tested using a Graduate Record Exam–style exam that measures verbal, analytical, mathematical, and technical abilities. Only the 25 highest-scoring applicants are chosen for each session. Tuition costs $2,400; financial assistance is available through a special low-interest loan program with Sallie Mae.

During the 6-month course, full-time classroom instruction is paired with the practical work experience the internships provide. The curriculum, offered in January, May, and September, has three parts, starting with 19 foundation subjects such as personal computer troubleshooting and an introduction to computer operating systems. The programming track includes instruction in C++, Visual Basic,

Oracle, and Java. The networking track includes training in Windows NT. The college's staff develops course subjects and instruction in consultation with the corporate sponsors. Students spend 3 months in classes that lead to specialization in either software programming or network administration. Then they spend another 3 months in paid, half-time internships, with the rest of their time spent in advanced computer training at the college. Representatives of sponsoring companies visit TRIP classes to talk about internships and job opportunities. Students can state their preferences for internships and companies and TRIP administrators do the matchmaking.

Approximately 10 employers currently partner with TRIP to offer internships, for which they agree to pay students between $12 and $15 an hour. Getting companies to participate by providing internships is crucial to the program's success. But NVCC's White said that the most critical challenge is attracting employers and encouraging them to offer internships to its students. Although more than 70% of companies responding to the George Mason University survey said they would be interested in partnering with educational institutions to help solve workforce development needs and fill job openings, employers may balk when asked to put real, paid work on the line. Business conditions may change, dictating whether companies can afford to offer paid internships or positions. In addition, many IT firms work under government contracts, which require special security clearances, specific levels of experience, or professional certifications that student interns probably lack.

The industry also is reluctant to take risks with novices, White admitted, particularly novices with no technology backgrounds. In addition, it is a corporate culture change to employ a TRIP student, a shift that some companies have difficulty getting used to. These interns are adults, not college kids. "These are people who have had a broad variety of life and work experiences, and it has required companies to be a little different in their hiring approaches," said David Hunn, director of the NVRP's Regional Workforce Development Coordinating Center. "[Employers] may need to realize they're looking at an alternative workforce, hiring someone who may be a little older than what they expect and with a work background that may be different than traditional employees. They must be willing to invest in a long-term outlook." To broaden its reach, TRIP is now trying to market the program to other employers with technology staff needs, like hospitals and banks, Hunn said. "The real work for us is getting the word out to companies that there is a workforce development program and another source of workers out here," he said.

Technology employers agree that labor shortages exist, but they do not always agree on how to solve the problem. The U.S. Department of Commerce's report suggested that companies often are not interested in training workers for high-tech jobs, preferring instead to compete for a limited pool of existing talent or to raid each other for the best talent. Short development cycles and product lives in the high-tech field contribute to some firms' reluctance to train, the report said. The report added that employers' reluctance to train is compounded by their fear that workers may leave for a job with a competitor before the training investment pays off.

Students in TRIP already have made the commitment to full-time study and training and already have paid for the training themselves, White pointed out. "Clearly, these students aren't looking for just another certificate or degree," Hunn said. "They're looking for a paying job in the high-tech field." This fact is an attractive one for many IT companies, White said. "If you look at this as a try-before-you-buy program, it actually is probably a less expensive strategy for companies than many job-referral bonus programs or other recruitment costs they incur otherwise," he said. Dynamic Technology Systems, for example, has come to rely on the program as an alternative source of interns and new employees. Of the nine TRIP interns the company has had so far, Dynamic Technology Systems has hired eight for full-time positions, said Orr. "I would recommend any HR person in IT explore these types of programs as another recruiting alternative," she said.

NEW ROUTE TO STAFFING

TRIP is not the only public–private partnership trying to solve the technology talent shortage through retraining and work opportunities, but it is one of the few that require full-time study and feature guaranteed internships. Hunn said that Nebraska, Delaware, Pennsylvania, and Maryland have showed interest in TRIP and the regional partnership as potential models for their own IT workforce programs. Companies that plan to get involved with a regional retraining program should make sure it includes both classroom-based training and on-the-job experience, Hunn said. Having the ability to give input on the academic course work and types of training most in demand to the business community is also important. Once a firm has committed to offering internships or temporary work, human resources staff should facilitate a work plan between the manager and the worker. "Outline a job plan that says specifically, 'Here's what you're going to do and here's what we're going to do,'" said Orr. Thinking of the arrangement as a potential temporary-to-permanent staffing situation also can help sell company leaders on the idea of giving technology novices a chance. "It may require a little more care and handling," said White, "but the outcome is going to be valuable in the long run."

The CATT'S Meow

Cecile S. Holmes

Global competition provides a basis for community colleges to help employers address unique training needs for technology. This case study documents such a program in South Carolina.

The Center for Accelerated Technology Training (CATT) is helping South Carolina compete in the global economy of the 21st century. Every time a new industry considers locating in South Carolina, it looks at a number of factors: property taxes, economic incentives, labor pool, and skill level of available employees. An ongoing program of the state's technical college system, CATT offers the sort of willing and able assistance to industry that can help South Carolina compete in the global economy of the 21st century.

Last year, 100 prospects worked with CATT at locations across the state in training and retraining programs for companies as diverse as insurance brokerage firms and electrical and electronic machinery manufacturers. In addition, CATT trained more than 4,500 employees for 94 different industries at sites from Anderson to North Charleston, South Carolina. "The bottom line … is that the level [needed] to compete in business and industry has been continually increasing," said Dr. James L. Hudgins, president of the state's technical college system. "Today, with the movement to a knowledge-based economy from a manufacturing-oriented one, a skilled workforce is a competitive advantage in recruiting industry.… A little short-term training no longer fits the bill." Instead, the technical colleges have refined and redefined their recruitment and training efforts.

Short-term training in what used to be called "special schools" made sense in the early 1960s, when the technical colleges first began in South Carolina. But today, a much more comprehensive approach is required. "Industry is depending on a much more highly skilled work force," Hudgins said. "Consequently, our colleges have evolved as businesses have changed."

CHIEF DRAWING CARD

In this high-tech era, South Carolina's technical college system remains one of the state's chief drawing cards for national and international industry. "Technical colleges provide an affordable opportunity for students to begin their college careers close to home and can be a stepping stone for students who desire a 4-year degree," according to Hudgins. According to a U.S. Department of Labor study titled "Workforce 2020: Work and Workers in the 21st Century," only about 20% of jobs today require a 4-year college degree. Approximately 65% of jobs require an associate degree or advanced training, whereas the remaining 15% require minimum skills.

Senator Ernest F. Hollings (D-SC), under whose watch as governor the state technical college system was launched in 1961, agrees that the system is a major magnet for industry. However, he worries that "we've got to have better planning strategically." South Carolina, he pointed out, is losing textile jobs when major firms find it cheaper to operate in Mexico or overseas. Part of the success of South Carolina's technical colleges springs from knowing how to marshal the necessary players to put together a strong recruitment effort. Essentials in that strategy are taught in courses offered through CATT. The statewide initiative offers special training in areas ranging from information technology to biotechnology. There is no cost to the business or industry where the employees will work; state dollars are used to train the workers.

RURAL IMPACTS

The impact of the state's technical program is felt even at the high school level in places like Williamsburg County, a poor rural area approximately 100 miles inland from Myrtle Beach and the state's prosperous Grand Strand. The unemployment rate nearly always hovers in the double digits in Williamsburg County where for decades, low-paying agricultural and manufacturing jobs were the main choices for local workers, even if they had high school diplomas. High school graduates faced the toughest decision: relocate elsewhere to earn a living wage or remain in the county where they grew up and face dismal employment prospects.

In the late 1990s, the Williamsburg County School District joined forces with Williamsburg Technical College to combat the problem. Nowadays in Kingstree, the county seat, the school district does not have a separate vocational school—it partners with the college to offer vocational training. An advisory committee includes local business leaders. "We have career fairs at which local businesses come to the high school," said Regina McKnight, district supervisor for career and technology education. "Students take a look at the programs, tour the tech campus, and then decide if they want to enroll."

Only 11th graders can qualify for the program. If they do, they enroll in courses in machine tool technology and industrial system technology at the technical college while still in high school. The school district also has a matriculation agreement with the technical college. "The technical college instructors and the high school teachers work together to determine the competencies those students must meet," McKnight said. If they are met, the students can earn technical college credit while still in high school. After graduation, vocational students in the machine tool and industrial system training programs often go to work at two of the county's major employers: Tupperware, based in Hemingway, and Peddinghaus, based in Andrews. Bringing about such custom-designed training helps both the county and the state attract new business and industry, according to Williamsburg Technical College President James C. Williamson.

MANY SUCCESSES

South Carolina's 16-college technical system, which attracts an estimated 90,000 students annually, recently celebrated its 41st birthday. It wins high praise from technical education leaders nationwide, despite the fact that the system faces significant challenges to keep pace with the current demands. This partnership linking economic development and technical education can boast of many successes. Examples include the German automaker BMW, which built a plant in South Carolina's "Upstate," and Hoffman-LaRoche, the pharmaceutical giant that constructed a plant in Florence.

A decade after BMW announced it would build its first North American plant in Spartanburg County, a study by the University of South Carolina's Moore School of Business revealed the enormous economic impact of the automaker on the state. Released in May 2002, the report said that through the so-called "multiplier effect," BMW supports 16,691 jobs statewide and accounts for $691 million in wages and salaries each year. "BMW is known worldwide as the ultimate driving machine," said Dr. Douglas P. Woodward, director of the study. "The results of our study make it clear BMW is an important economic development driver, as well."

CATT has lured other companies to the Upstate in recent months, said Ben Dillard, vice president for economic development and continuing education at Greenville Technical College. Greenville is the state's largest and oldest technical school, with 11,000 students and a network of satellite campuses. CATT plays a critical role, said Dillard, because it is "a link between the technical college, which is the resource group, and the business or new industry. CATT has the ability to find the resource and bring it to that expanded or new business coming into town. And CATT provides the same service, whether it's for a three- or four-man shop or a major company like BMW."

Within the past year, at least nine different firms in the area have turned to CATT and Greenville Technical College to assist with training or retraining. The companies range from an auto warehouse distributor to a firm specializing in textile specialty weaving. After working with CATT, other firms, ranging from a rubber belt and hose manufacturer to a food packaging company, have announced their intent to create more than 230 new jobs in Greenville County.

Steve Taylor, a Greenville native who is now human resources manager for a lock-manufacturing company called CompX National in Mauldin, South Carolina, said Greenville and the CATT program (or its predecessor, "Special Schools") have proven essential to his firm. In fact, CompX has financed a scholarship for a student in Greenville Tech's machine tool technology program for some 15 years. "They have been a key to us in the start up," said Taylor, whose company employs 375 people. Two years ago, CompX purchased another lock-manufacturing company that was going out of business in Wisconsin. "Although there were some similarities [in our products], there were also some differences," Taylor said. "Greenville Tech helped us coordinate training classes, on-the-job training, and one-on-one teaching. We probably trained and developed 80 people for this new product line in our business."

Thomas E. Barton, Jr., president of Greenville Technical College, called the CATT program "a team effort that has put this state way ahead" of most southern states. South Carolina is in serious competition with other states in the Sunbelt determined to attract new industry. "What do we have to assist us in winning this battle?" Barton asked. "We simply tell them, 'We will give you whatever you need to get you into production. We'll supply you with the skilled workers who can help you compete in the global marketplace.'" At that point, conceded Barton, "that's a simple statement to make. But we have a tremendous track record on delivering. I've been with it for 40 years, and I've never seen a single project fail yet statewide."

NOT JUST THE UPSTATE

The Upstate is not the only region that has been successful in convincing industry to locate in its area. In 2000, Williamsburg County in east central South Carolina, where almost one third of the 37,000 residents live below the poverty line, attracted a service center for ClientLogic, a Nashville, Tennessee–based firm that specializes in customer service and technical support for e-commerce and technology firms. ClientLogic now employs more than 400 workers at its customer contact center in the county. Its advent, and the addition of $10-an-hour jobs, offers hope in a place where many workers still travel 2 hours by bus each way to work as maids, waiters, and waitresses at Grand Strand hotels.

In South Carolina's Low Country, technical colleges are also "a very integral part of our community and a respected resource in our region," according to David T. Ginn, head of the Charleston Development Alliance and immediate past president of the South Carolina Economic Developers Association. "The technical college system and the training system have been phenomenal for this state's growth and its history." Without technical colleges, high-tech industries would not have moved into southeastern states such as North Carolina and South Carolina, said George B. Vaughan, a professor at North Carolina State University and former president of two community colleges in Virginia. "These schools have made it possible for literally millions of citizens to develop their talents and learn things they would not have learned otherwise," Vaughan said. "By opening access [to education], we've tapped into talent we didn't know we had—minorities, women, lower socioeconomic groups that would have been denied an education."

In the case of Williamsburg County, ClientLogic Chief Executive Officer Mark Briggs called the tech school partnership a driving force behind the company's decision to locate there. That alliance united Williamsburg Technical College with a local economic board that included civic, religious, and political leaders. "I thought it would be a way in which we would perhaps alleviate some of the poverty in Williamsburg County," said the Reverend Franklin Garrett, pastor of Bethesda United Methodist Church. "If we could do that, we would be much better off." Industrial, educational, and political leaders say such hospitality helps bring in new firms. Other states may offer tax incentives, but few can promise new businesses a custom-trained labor force ready to work.

Note. From "The CATT's Meow," by C. S. Holmes, 2003, *Business & Economic Review, 49*(3), pp. 19–22. Copyright 2003 by Cecile S. Holmes. Adapted with permission.

Banking Consortium Cashes in on State Funding

Jana Bowers

Some people erroneously believe that most community college training is geared to meeting the needs of manufacturers or information technology employers. This case study documents an effort to help banks, key to financial services, meet their training needs.

In the summers after high school and while attending college, I worked as a part-time employee for Morris County National Bank in Naples, Texas, and then for the State Bank of Omaha in Omaha, Texas. During the time I was employed at the State Bank of Omaha, I had the opportunity to meet Brantley Foster, a Texas Ranger for the Northeast Texas area. The occasion was not a pleasant one, as he interviewed me just after the bank had been robbed. This robbery occurred quite a few years ago, and the bank was robbed once more while I was employed there. I shall never forget those experiences.

Brantley Foster is now retired and is chief of security for Guaranty Bank. In the fall of 1999, Chief Foster and I met once again to discuss some security training for local bankers. I was excited about assisting Chief Foster with this training. Now, almost 18 months later, a banking consortium has been formed and a grant for $343,522 has been funded for Northeast Texas Community College (NTCC), Mount Pleasant, Texas, and 10 local banks in our nine-county service delivery. The NTCC Skills Development Program, the Banking Consortium, and the Texas Workforce Commission work together to provide customized training to the Northeast Texas financial institutions.

Customized Training

In 1996, the Texas legislature appropriated $25 million for the Skills Development Fund to assist community and technical colleges in responding to the needs of businesses, to help create new jobs through business expansion or relocation, and to continue to help create a competitive and trained Texas workforce. The Skills Development Program at NTCC was one of the first programs funded by the Texas Workforce Commission. The Skills Development Program parallels the mission of the college in that "education is a lifetime right." This program at NTCC provides workforce education courses and training in specific semiskilled and skilled occupations to 19 businesses and industries in the nine-county service delivery area.

Since the inception of the Skills Development Program, NTCC has been awarded more than $1.6 million in grant funds offered by the Texas Workforce Commission to provide customized training to 1,628 employees through five grants with 19 business partners. On May 31, 2000, the Texas Workforce Commission awarded more than $343,000 to NTCC and 10 area financial institutions with a skills development grant to provide customized training to 335 employees for an 18-month period.

Course Variety

The courses listed in the grant covered areas such as bank accounting, bank security/robbery, individual retirement account (IRA) administration, principles of banking, Internet banking, IRA introduction, money and banking, operational compliance, basic and advanced teller training, basic and advanced computer training, and conversational Spanish. A project advisory committee was formed consisting of a contact person from each financial institution. This committee meets on a regular basis and is active in deciding the banking curriculum and scheduling the consortium. The project advisory committee was instrumental in approving a 1-year business administration banking certificate and a 2-year business administration banking specialization (associate of applied science) degree for the college.

The instructional staff for the banking consortium consists of full-time and adjunct faculty of NTCC. These instructors have been innovative in the development and implementation of the curriculum. The banks in the consortium leased a tour bus to take 80 students and other banking personnel to Dallas to tour the Federal Reserve Bank as part of the money and banking credit course. Earlier in the year, an 8-hour bank robbery/security seminar was planned; 155 employees of the consortium attended. The seminar was held between the regular semesters and was taught by two professionals: Deborah Brown, chief of police of Southwestern University in Georgetown, and Harold Eavenson, sheriff of Rockwall County.

To meet the ever-changing requirements of the banking industry, an 8-hour operational compliance seminar was conducted; 41 employees from the banking consortium attended. By offering this seminar, employees of the consortium were able to learn about the changes to the banking industry and to implement changes before the deadline created by the passage of a new law affecting the industry. "The banking consortium has been a great benefit for Guaranty Bank," says Clifton A. Payne, executive vice president and chief financial officer. "This program is providing quality training close to home that otherwise would have only been offered out of town. The program affords our employees the opportunity to enhance their education while providing the bank with more knowledgeable employees."

Note. From "Banking Consortium Cashes in on Rewards of State Funding," by J. Bowers, 2001, *Texas Banking, 90*(6), pp. 16–17. Copyright 2001 by Texas Banking. Adapted with permission.

CASE 7

Job-Readiness Program Is a Win–Win in Atlantic City

Nancy Wong

Community colleges play an important role in helping casinos meet their training needs. This case study documents such a program, providing trained talent for entry-level workers.

For 28-year-old Patricia James, the most exciting thing among the glitter and thrill of casinos on Atlantic City's boardwalk is her new job at Harrah's. Patricia had been unemployed and collecting public assistance for a little more than a year. "I was looking for a job on a day-to-day basis," she said. She also spent her time caring for her 8-year-old son, Eric. As a single mother without a high school diploma, Patricia's job search was a difficult one—that is, until earlier this year, when Patricia's caseworker encouraged her to enroll in a new program called Atlantic City First (AC First).

A month-long job readiness course for welfare recipients, AC First is the result of a partnership between Atlantic Cape Community College (ACCC) and the human resources departments at several of Atlantic City's hospitality industries, including Harrah's Casino Hotel and Mirage Resorts. "The program teaches [participants] how to apply for a job, how to be more responsible, how to fill out job applications correctly, and how to prepare a résumé," Patricia explained. "And it not only teaches you how to get a job, but how to keep a job." AC First teaches job skills for long-term success.

In March 1999, 40 students attended the first session of AC First at ACCC in Atlantic City. Participants were referred by caseworkers from Temporary Assistance to Needy Families (TANF), a state-run organization that assists low-income families, particularly targeting single mothers. AC First students go through 4 weeks of basic skills training, including computer instruction and job-development consultation. They are taught by several teachers and speakers, including members of the human resources staff at Harrah's and other companies in the partnership. During the final week of the program, students work 20 hours at community-based service projects at ACCC and a variety of sites. Throughout this process, students learn to identify acceptable and unacceptable attitudes to carry into the workplace.

The Harrah's human resources department trains AC First supervisors on how to support and coach the welfare population, orient the new employees to the workplace, and report back to the AC First job counselors if problems occur. The human resources department's primary role in the program is to support communication between the college, the students, and their supervisors. To get hired, program graduates go to special AC First job fairs and undergo the same procedures as any other job candidate. "We haven't changed our employment standards," said Jan Ellison, vice president of human resources at Harrah's and a main supporter of AC First. "Candidates are required to be drug tested, and we have assessments to make sure they're well-suited for work in the service industry. These individuals are passing our standards, which is a big positive."

Patricia graduated with the first cycle of AC First students, and only a week later, she was hired as a guest service representative for the front desk at Harrah's. The company also hired five other people from the same group for different positions. "The things that kept me from getting ahead were my fear of change and the obstacles of being unemployed," said Patricia. But AC First taught her how to overcome those challenges. "Now I know I can achieve my goals and do what I need to do to reach them. I apply the skills I learned every day."

Teaching people to use and broaden their skills is precisely what the program was designed to do. "Welfare reform isn't a simple process of no longer giving someone a check—that doesn't solve the problem," said Ellison. "And I personally wanted to make a difference in that area." And AC First definitely has made a difference for Patricia. Now with a high school equivalency degree on the way and more confidence in her step, she has made her family proud. She said, "My son is so excited that I have a job now especially because it's at Harrah's!"

Note. From "Job-Readiness Program Is a 'Win–Win' in Atlantic City," by N. Wong, 1999, *Workforce Management, 78*(6), p. 152. Copyright 1992–2004 by Crain Communications, Inc. Adapted with permission.

CASE 8

Atlantic Cape Community College: Working Closely With the Workforce Investment Board

Patricia A. Owens

Here is another case study that documents the role played by community colleges in addressing the training needs of employers in the gaming industry.

Atlantic Cape Community College (ACCC), the Atlantic Cape May Workforce Investment Board (WIB), and the major gaming/hospitality industry employers have been working effectively together in the Atlantic City Casino Training Consortium since the mid-1990s. The partnership began when several human resource executives in the casino industry realized that the New Jersey Department of Labor's (DOL) customized training contracts, into which all employers pay through the unemployment fund, could contribute a significant amount of workforce training funds. The industry was facing a decade of unparalleled growth, and employers were worried that they would not find the local talent they needed to realize expansion dreams. This highly competitive industry was willing to put differences aside to work together to find the labor pool it needed and to allow the local community college, ACCC, to broker the deal to the state.

ACCC, working closely with the area's WIB, devised a proposal to the state to help move people who were on welfare or were chronically underemployed and unemployed into the labor force. Adapting a proven curriculum model from another state, ACCC was able to land the first major state customized training contract, Atlantic City First Job Readiness Program (AC First) in 1998. AC First was a two-year $1.2 million contract with ACCC as the training provider and three area casino properties as partners who committed to hiring the program's completers. At the end of the contract, AC First had not only met proposal goals but also had exceeded everyone's expectations. Of the 963 hard-to-place adults enrolled, 656 had completed the training. Of these, 463 were placed in full-time positions with the three employer partners and several other properties who had asked to be included in the recruitment and training effort. The program was able to leverage an additional $804,000 in matching contracts and in-kind donations and to garner accolades from the employers, WIB, social service agencies, and the state.

With an expanded consortium of employers, the college—again with the WIB's endorsement and support—approached the state for a renewal. South Jersey Hospitality Opportunities for Potential Employees (SJ HOPE) was funded by the NJ DOL for $1.9 million over 24 months. The job readiness program expanded to include transitioning ex-offenders, newly arrived immigrants, specific outreach and training for Latina Temporary Assistance for Needy Families (TANF) recipients, and career advancement training and support for front line casino workers. SJ HOPE's employer base now included 11 of the 12 existing casino properties. Apparently, human resource executives were eager to lower their hiring risk by bringing on trained and job-ready workers. Several HR executives tracked the retention of workers given training services against those not given an opportunity to train. Not surprisingly, they found a significant reduction in turnover rates for those groomed with training services. In addition, Caesars Atlantic City renovated a space next to its training center for a jointly sponsored classroom/computer lab run by ACCC. This employer-based learning center provided a convenient hub for the program's incumbent worker training and continues to exist as a joint effort 5 years after SJ HOPE ended.

At the conclusion of the SJ HOPE workforce development program, 720 potential workers had been enrolled, and 560 graduated with 420 placed in jobs in the casino industry. Another 600 additional workers were trained in customer service skills; 105 incumbent workers at three properties were trained in a pilot career ladder program (and subsequently promoted); and an additional 1,351 incumbent workers were trained in technology skills at the learning center.

Buoyed by its success, the Atlantic City Casino Training Consortium expanded its applications to include a DOL grant for a sectoral planning initiative to enhance regional recruitment efforts. The consortium captured another DOL grant to uptrain 44 incumbent Spanish-speaking kitchen workers in culinary skills and accomplish 12 credits at ACCC's Academy of Culinary Arts (again with commitments for advancement and wage increases by the industry). This bilingual culinary program was recognized by DOL as a best practice at its 2005 national workforce development conference in Philadelphia.

The Atlantic City Casino Training Consortium continues to capture millions in public dollars through customized training contracts, literacy grants, and workforce development training funds for both potential and incumbent workers. The community college remains the critical lynchpin in the collaborative, providing technical assistance, grant-writing expertise, executive leadership, and "lingo" translation services for both the employers and the public sector. In fact, the model has worked so well that the WIB replicated the framework to fit the area's emerging retail industry, resulting in a public–private–higher education collaboration called Institute for Service Excellence (ISE). The ISE is opening in December 2006 at the Hamilton Mall to provide free sales and service training and job placement services. The partners include Atlantic Cape May WIB, ACCC (managing partner), Kravco-Simon Developers, the New Jersey Department of Labor and Workforce Development, the National Retail Federation, and the Casino Reinvestment Development Authority.

And, the WIB-led collaboration-building has not stopped there. Last year, the WIB, ACCC, and area health-care employers were successful in capturing a $1.2 million award from the U.S. Department of Commerce Economic Development Administration, which was matched by another $1.8 million in state and local public funds to renovate the ACCC Atlantic City campus for a Health Professional Institute (HPI). HPI is focused on training allied and auxiliary health-care workers for the rapidly expanding health-care industry in Southern New Jersey. This award followed a $.5 million planning grant from Robert Wood Johnson New Jersey Health Initiatives to address the critical shortage of nurses in the area.

The following are considered to be key factors in successful collaborative workforce development programs. The collaboration must be

- **Employer led.** Employers need to articulate their training and workforce development needs and programs must be responsive to those specific needs. In other words, cookie cutter approaches do not work for the long haul.
- **Union supported.** All the industries for which this collaborative approach worked were highly unionized. The partners worked hard to include union officials and ensured that training programs provided added-value benefits to the union, like helping expose potential workers to union jobs and working closely with the unions for incumbent worker training.
- **One Stop–centered.** The WIB acted as an independent coordinator and convener. It was able to bring all the stakeholders to the table and support industry-wide approaches.
- **Able to acquire translation services.** ACCC acted as the translator between the public and private sectors by interpreting government regulations and requirements to employers and modifying business lingo to fit WIA and other funding stream requirements and benchmarks. This technical assistance was invaluable to the continued nurturing of the consortiums.
- **Demand driven.** ACCC created curricula to meet employers' and workers' skill demands. The college did not bring canned curriculum to the table or try to fit worker needs into a static syllabus.

- **Willing to creatively use existing funding streams.** The collaborative looked to match, leverage, and creatively adjust its programs and demands to take advantage of public and private funding opportunities.
- **Able to leverage publicly supported higher education.** The collaborative recognized that the publicly funded community college was the appropriate vehicle to most effectively address its training requirements, and oftentimes employers worked exclusively with the community college to handle workforce development needs.

WEDnetPA: The Creation of the Workforce and Economic Development Network of Pennsylvania

Patrick E. Gerity, Larry Michael, and Tom Venditti

This case study chronicles the creation of a very successful alliance of 33 diverse educational providers. These providers include 14 community colleges in regions throughout the state, which coordinate the resources of the entire network and serve as points of contact for qualified companies in Pennsylvania that are eligible to receive funding through the Pennsylvania Department of Community and Economic Development's Guaranteed Free Training program.

PROPOSAL RESPONSE AND DEVELOPMENT

In August 1998, the Pennsylvania Department of Community and Economic Development (DCED) issued a request for proposals (RFPs) from individual colleges, community colleges, and universities or consortiums of schools to deliver Pennsylvania's new Guaranteed Free Training (GFT) program for a 2-year period. The $9 million in funding provided by DCED was designated for training newly hired Pennsylvania-resident employees in manufacturing and technology-based businesses.

The Pennsylvania State System of Higher Education (PA State System) invited the Pennsylvania Commission for Community Colleges (PCCC) to collaborate on a proposal to form a consortium among the 14 community colleges and the 14 state-owned universities to deliver the GFT program. The proposed consortium, the Workforce and Economic Development Network of Pennsylvania (WEDnetPA), would act as a collaborative partnership across the state and would provide workforce and economic development support to the commonwealth through the new GFT program for new and expanding businesses. Charles Clevenger and Patrick Gerity represented the PA State System. The late Lee Myers and his assistant, Dan Stark, represented PCCC. It was agreed that Gerity and Stark would develop the proposal and that the PA State System would be the designated recipient and manager of the $9 million funding, if the contract were awarded.

APPROVAL AND START-UP

The proposal was awarded in January 1999. Upon the recommendation of DCED to include a technical college in the consortium, to strengthen coverage for the middle and northern tier of Pennsylvania, the Pennsylvania College of Technology was added as a WEDnetPA partner. With the consortium formed, the first step taken for start-up was to pull together the WEDnetPA Action Team to develop a strategic action plan. All but one member of the Action Team were the same people who had reviewed the proposal in before it was submitted:

- Patrick Gerity and Charles Clevenger from the PA State System
- Dan Stark and Lee Myers from PCCC
- Jack Mahon, assistant to the president at Reading Area Community College
- Mark Borger, director of workforce development at Harrisburg Area Community College
- Paul Pierpoint, dean of business and industry programs for Northampton Area Community College
- Paul Gentile, dean of workforce development at the Community College of Allegheny County
- Larry Michael, dean of workforce development at the Pennsylvania College of Technology

The Action Team met the first week of February 1999 to begin development of the WEDnetPA framework, structure, guidelines, processes, and procedures to implement the GFT program. Afterward, the team would meet biweekly, with the intent of meeting a kick-off date in mid-March: The commonwealth was very anxious to get this program up and running. As meetings progressed, however, it became clear that more time was needed to review guidelines and contracting procedures and to develop marketing pieces. The kick-off date was postponed to April 19. The decision to postpone proved to be wise. The team continued its work, which enabled it to meet its goal of ensuring a speedy GFT application process.

The Action Team was very wise in constructing the budget. It set aside significant funds to develop high-quality marketing materials to promote the GFT program. A value-added feature of WEDnetPA's proposal was to set up, via the Internet, a statewide application approval process that would cut down the project approval time to 5 business days or less. Once this online application was up and running, the goal was to reduce approval time to approximately 3 business days. This showed the consortium's serious intent to respond in real business time to business clients.

Once the team was satisfied with the guidelines and policies developed, the next step was to have the PA State System's legal counsel review all of the contracts, eligibility forms, contracting and subcontracting forms, application forms, and memoranda of understanding to ensure that they complied with the legal requirements of both the PA State System and the Commonwealth of Pennsylvania. The Action Team recognized the critical need to show that all business transactions conducted by WEDnetPA should be accountable and audit-proof.

With guidelines, applications, and marketing materials approved and in place, a kick-off date was established to invite all of the presidents of the community colleges, state universities, and the Pennsylvania College of Technology to attend the first partners' meeting. The team invited Michael Taggart to be the keynote speaker. Taggart had established the Enterprise Ohio Network and had acted as a consultant to the WEDnetPA Action Team. Taggart agreed to share his experience with and knowledge of managing a larger statewide network with WEDnetPA in addition to delivering the keynote address, in which he would focus on developing collaboration within a network.

CONTINUED GROWTH

Over the next several years, WEDnetPA continued to evolve, building its brand and securing its position as Pennsylvania's preeminent incumbent workforce training program. With this success came increased state funding and the need to bring on additional partners to fully serve all regions of the Commonwealth. By FY 2003–2004, the network added six new partners and reached an annual funding level of $21.5 million. The program also added an online training option allowing for "just in time" and "just enough" educational opportunities. Among other things, online training would include basic skills, professional development, and information technology training that could be structured as a single course or an entire online library.

In addition to providing access to training funds, WEDnetPA envisioned itself as a resource for training information. The online Workplace Learning Resource Center was developed and incorporated into the network's Web site, giving employers the tools they needed to get the most from the program and to maximize the potential of their companies. The Center, and its companion Education and Training Resource Guide, provided references for better business practices, sample training plans, and guidelines on linking these plans to business goals. As the Center continued to evolve, it began to serve as a common portal through which the WEDnetPA partners could market the program and offer their entire client base access to valuable training resources. Each partner portal was customized from a standard template to give the appearance of individual ownership, while providing easy access to a wealth of information stored on a common server.

The WEDnetPA partners were continually mindful of the need to be efficient and responsive to business needs. In FY 2004–2005, a paperless contracting system was developed and successfully tested. The following year, all WEDnetPA partners began to submit grant requests and receive approved contracts entirely online. This further improved the response time of the program and allowed the partners to focus on other more important aspects of the program.

FY 2005–2006 was a year of positive reorganization. A transition in leadership occurred at several levels. The beginning of the fiscal year ushered in a new statewide director and witnessed a smooth and successful transition in leadership at DCED. Perhaps more importantly, there was also a shift in responsibility for program administration from the PA State System to Pennsylvania College of Technology, which brought with it the relocation of the statewide office. Despite all of these significant changes, the WEDnetPA partners remained focused and committed to delivering a high-quality workforce training program.

In fact, it was through this period of reorganization that the network began to revisit and strengthen its ties to other local, regional, and statewide workforce and economic development organizations. Demand for the GFT program outpaced the grant funds available at a rate of three to one. While there was always an expectation that the WEDnetPA partners would seek local input to help prioritize and rank GFT applications, improved communications helped to ensure collaboration with these vital partners, especially local Workforce Investment Boards (WIBs).

WEDnetPA partners worked closely with their local WIBs to identify regional priorities and target GFT funds to support their objectives. Partners received letters of support from their WIBs describing efforts to collaborate and align resources. The WIBs and other members of the workforce and economic development community also participated in the review and prioritization of GFT applications. There was a clear improvement in the outcomes of these efforts when compared to previous fiscal years.

As a result, WEDnetPA was now more closely aligned with the objectives and strategies of the Pennsylvania Department of Labor and Industry (L&I). Steps were taken to align GFT funds with L&I's Industry Partnership Worker Training funds, which support collaborative industry partnership (consortia) training efforts. This helps to achieve opportunities and efficiencies that could not be realized through the single-company application process. Following extensive discussions with both DCED and L&I, WEDnetPA created a special set-aside of funds to support consortia applications.

As we look ahead, the WEDnetPA partners recognize the importance of understanding how to measure the Commonwealth's return on the investments (ROI) made in the GFT program and made this the focus of a special initiative in FY 2006–2007. An Action Team subcommittee was formed to evaluate methods to calculate ROI and to conduct a pilot among a number of companies. Once a refined procedure has been developed, it will be more widely implemented across the program and will provide important feedback relative to the overall impact of the GFT program.

WEDnetPA is working with DCED to explore other statewide training priorities and to evaluate the potential of targeting additional funds to address these needs. While the GFT program is the hallmark of the network today, the future holds great promise. The proven ability and effectiveness of the WEDnetPA partnership has the potential and capacity to uniquely serve the Commonwealth's workforce training agenda for many years to come.

REASONS FOR SUCCESS

WEDnetPA's Action Team and partners can be credited with much of the consortium's success. The team was very productive and collaborative from the start, most of its members had known one another, and collectively they brought many years of workforce and economic development experience to the project. The partners include representatives from the PA State System (four members), community colleges (four members), and Pennsylvania College of Technology (one member). Due to the early expansion of WEDnetPA, an "other" category was created for new partners (two members). The WEDnetPA director, fiscal agent, and technical support representative also attend the Action Team meetings. In addition to the Action Team, WEDnetPA created an Executive Committee whose members include two executives from community colleges, two from the PA State System, one "other" executive, a manager from DCED, and the WEDnetPA director and fiscal Agent. The Executive Committee deals with policy and funding issues along with planning the future of WEDnetPA. These two organizational initiatives have guided WEDnetPA through its 8 years of existence.

At the end of the first year, WEDnetPA conducted its first partners' retreat, inviting all partners to participate in a two-and-a-half-day workshop during which they reviewed the guidelines, engaged in professional development and team-building activities, attended DCED presentations, and took an annual certification exam. The annual partners' retreat has been very successful in improving the WEDnetPA partners' performance.

Finally, another important element contributing to the success of WEDnetPA in its development is the commitment demonstrated by the following professionals: James McCormick, chancellor of the PA State System; Lee Myers, executive director of PCCC; Davey Gilmour, president of Pennsylvania College of Technology;

and Sam McCullough, secretary of DCED. These leaders were totally in agreement to collaborate in the development of WEDnetPA. Their support enabled WEDnetPA to get off to a very successful start, and their continued support through the early years enabled WEDnetPA to become the largest and most effective incumbent workforce development program in Pennsylvania. In its first 8 years, WEDnetPA has trained 669,860 workers, served 11,322 companies, and completed 16,647 contracts for training in Pennsylvania.

PART 2

Case Studies of Community College Business Consulting

A less-well-known role that community colleges play is to provide support for local businesses when they have need of business consulting, a growth field. The cases that illustrate this role are as follows.

Case 10. Niagara County Community College Center Helps Small Businesses Get Rolling

Case 11. Community Colleges in the Lead With Homeland Security

Case 12. Community College, University, and Corporate Partnership to Combat Employment Shortages

Niagara County Community College Center Helps Small Businesses Get Rolling

Joe Iannarelli

Community colleges play an important role in offering more than training to business. This case study documents a role played by one community college in offering business consulting services to local small businesses, a key driver in employment and in economic development for many communities.

Tucked away on the Sanborn campus of Niagara County Community College (NCCC) is a resource small businesses use for just about everything. One of the first formal business development centers in the state, the NCCC Small Business Development Center was formed 18 years ago. "The mission and goal is always the same," said Richard Gorko, executive director. "We must advise, counsel, and assist small business development any way we can. They all come to us with an idea."

RECORD OF SUCCESS

The U.S. Small Business Administration provides funding for the NCCC Small Business Development Center, which is similar to those in other parts of western New York. Each center's success is based on the number of clients served annually, economic impact, and jobs created and retained, along with training events held to educate entrepreneurs. In the 1999–2000 program year, the Niagara center worked with 726 clients, helped retain 163 jobs, created 265 jobs, garnered $14 million in investments, and held 30 training events with 1,300 attendees. The center has access to the International Trade Center Small Business Development

Center, which is also in Niagara Falls. That center serves as a trade venue and domestic assistance office. An outreach center, located on the campus of Genesee State College, broadens the Niagara center's reach to nine combined employees. Small business development centers also are tied to education. The Niagara center can tap into the resources available at the community college, as well as a sister center at Buffalo State College. Small business development centers consider a business with 500 or fewer employees to be a small business. Ninety percent of businesses in Niagara County fall under this classification.

DIVERSE CLIENTELE

Clients are not just from Niagara County. Assistance has been offered to those in Erie, Orleans, and Genesee counties. The center participates in a self-employment assistance program through the New York Department of Labor and works with the Niagara County Industrial Development Agency (IDA) to implement a microenterprise program. The IDA program offers up to $25,000 in seed capital after a 12-week training program.

For restaurant owner Jack Soldano, the center is a valuable promotional tool. His establishment, Villa Fortunata's of Lewiston, caters to patrons from all over the world at the height of the tourist season. "Lewiston is an area that sells itself in the summer with Artpark and other attractions," he said. "In the winter, people tend to stay away or disappear. Most small businesses try to promote everything in this area so people come year round. The center helps promote the area as much as they can. Every little bit helps when people come in through the door. We are always trying to figure out ways to bring people into Lewiston. All the restaurants in Lewiston are known for what they sell."

Through the center's influence, the restaurant participated in "A Taste of Buffalo" last year—winning an award at the popular food festival. When it came time for the "Taste of Lewiston," Villa Fortunata's lived up to its popularity, winning another award. "You sell yourself, especially in the restaurant business," Soldano said. "Those events helped spread the word about us and Lewiston. Lewiston is not closed for the winter. Artpark is a tremendous year-round attraction. People always talk about promotion, especially for the people that live here."

When it came time for Fayyaz Hussain to put together a loan package for his company to expand, he called the center for help. "Loan packages are like walking through a maze," he said. "It's even more beneficial for people that really need the help. It was critical for us. For any new company, it's a must. It's tough for small businesses because you have to deal with all different kinds of agencies. That takes a lot of time and causes a lot of headaches." Hussain is president of Farmis Inc., doing business as United Biochemicals, a manufacturer of specialty products for the biotechnology industry. With seven employees, the company moved into a new 23,000-square-foot facility in June 2002 at the Inducon International Commerce park in Sanborn. "When we started the project, the center was very helpful in getting our package together," Hussain said. "That saved us a lot of time. It would have taken a lot longer than we would have hoped without them. The loan approval process did take some time, but the center put us in touch with various financial lenders so we would go to the right place."

The same holds true for Michael Klock, president of the Niagara Sports Arena, a recreational in-line skating rink and complex in Olcott. "I wanted to fill a void in rural Niagara County," he said. "The center helped us with everything. The building was dilapidated and needed major repairs that required more capital (than) my wife, Susan, and I were able to front." The Klocks purchased the complex in May 2000. Participation has nearly tripled with the addition of adult leagues and multiple uses for soccer and lacrosse. "We needed some direction and financial planning assistance," Klock said. "They helped us develop a marketing campaign and an entire business plan. We could not have done it without them. I would have been overwhelmed."

BROAD-BASED INFLUENCE

The Niagara center works hand-in-hand with various business development agencies in Niagara County. "The chambers of commerce in general have had an excellent working relationship with the center," said David Kinyon, former president of the Eastern Niagara Chamber of Commerce and executive vice president of Niagara USA Chamber of Commerce. "They have been an integral partner in small business formation efforts. It's a level of sophistication that the chambers of commerce don't have, along with devoting the right amount of time and attention to small business development. They are a key partner in the entire region's economic development strategy."

The Niagara County IDA often sends some of its customers to the center. They are either seeking loans or developing business plans. "It allows for continuity in assistance and business plan development," said John Simon, executive director of the IDA. "That is very helpful to us. They are able to provide professional assistance for start-up businesses along with well-established companies. They do a fine job." That job appears to have left a lasting impression. "We do a great job of keeping the best things secret in Niagara County," said Robert Newman, president and chief executive officer of the Niagara USA Chamber of Commerce. "The center should be at the forefront of everything. A lot of people use their resources in one way or another. There are very few places where you can find services like that. The real growth in this economy is small business."

Note. From "NCCC Center Helps Small Businesses Get Rolling," by J. Iannarelli, 2002, *Business First*, 18(35), p. 21. Copyright 2002 by American City Business Journals, Inc. Adapted with permission.

CASE *11*

Community Colleges in the Lead With Homeland Security

Marilyn Gilroy

Community colleges play a responsive role in U.S. government policy. This case study documents a program in which a community college helps meet an important homeland security need.

S ince September 11, 2001, the term *homeland security* has entered the nation's vocabulary and is now becoming part of the curriculum at hundreds of colleges and universities. Courses such as "Hazardous Materials Emergency Response," "Training for Mass Fatalities," and "Understanding Terrorism Risks" can be found on many campuses now. No sector of higher education is responding faster to the need for homeland security–related training than community colleges, which have begun offering degree and certificate programs and building new facilities.

OWENS COMMUNITY COLLEGE, OHIO

Owens Community College (OCC), near Toledo, Ohio, broke ground in the spring of 2005 for its $10 million center featuring an antiterrorism simulation center. The Fire and Police Training Center for Professional Development and Homeland Security, located on a 110-acre site, will feature a command and simulation center for regional antiterrorism and emergency management plus state-of-the-art classrooms and laboratories. When Michael Brown, then-undersecretary of the Federal Emergency Management Agency (FEMA) of the Department of

Homeland Security, visited the campus in June 2005 and reviewed the plans, he called the center "the best in the country." But he also used the occasion to remind audience members of Northwest Ohio's susceptibility to terrorist attacks, citing the proximity of Toledo to the international border of Canada, the region's immediacy to the coast of Lake Erie, and the heavy flow of trucks that criss-cross the area's interstates. Consequently, OCC feels a special obligation to contribute to homeland security efforts. "We're not looking at this [center] as a business decision," said Paul Unger, provost of OCC. "We're looking at this as a duty."

The center includes advanced technologies that make new partnerships possible and reduce costs for training the security workforce. The technology, provided by Ohio's Third Frontier Network (TFN), links OCC, the University of Findlay, and a consortium of other institutions to area police, fire, and emergency personnel for seminars, consultation, and equipment demonstrations. By using fiber-optic cable connected to computerized video that operates on dedicated, secure channels for emergency management, the system allows real-time observations of training exercises from remote locations. The network enables fire and police departments to conduct "hands-on" exercises, via distance learning, on a variety of simulated terrorist incidents, emergency hazards, and natural disasters. "The application of the Third Frontier Network to homeland security training will put Ohio on the cutting edge," said Unger.

OCC is strongly positioned in its efforts to increase antiterrorism programs. The college has a longstanding commitment to regional training for safety forces, including an agreement with the Ohio Fire Academy to provide college course work to full- and part-time firefighters throughout the state. This collaboration enables fire academy students to earn an associate degree while simultaneously receiving instructional and laboratory training. OCC currently offers associate degrees and certificate programs in fire science technology and criminal justice science technology, as well as emergency medical technician certification. Courses offered within the public service curricula include criminal law and procedure, patrol operations, crime scene processing, firefighting tactics and command, hazardous materials, fire inspection principles, and first responder. "We are taking every step possible to provide the highest level training to emergency service personnel," said Unger.

FAIRMONT STATE COMMUNITY AND TECHNICAL COLLEGE, WEST VIRGINIA

Other community colleges are using existing curricula to expand into counterterrorism degree programs. Fairmont State Community and Technical College (FSC&TC), West Virginia, offers an associate of applied science degree in homeland security with separate tracks in aviation, criminal justice, emergency management, and safety. Amy Baker, director of public relations, said that all four tracks have a common core curriculum to allow for cross-training among the fields, which is the workforce standard.

The program was developed through a 7-month process, including the input of an advisory committee with members representing federal and state government agencies and private industry. The process moved quickly, said Baker, because of the college's existing personnel and resources such as its Robert C. Byrd National Aerospace Education Center.

"No new faculty were required for us to be able to offer these courses," said Baker. "We have existing programs in criminal justice, safety, EMS, and aviation, so we drew from these resources."

The degree program began accepting applicants in 2003 and already has 20 full-time students and a growing part-time enrollment. The first graduates completed their studies in December 2004. "This program was a major accomplishment," said Rich McCormick, assistant provost for FSC&TC. "We believe we were the first community college in the nation to offer an associate degree program with four tracks. In our research, we found no other programs like this one, and that helped us be more creative in our design."

This unique program, which is listed with FEMA and state law enforcement agencies, requires students to pass a criminal background check because of the sensitive information involved in their course work and the nature of their employment. Students also must meet FSC&TC's admissions requirements. Graduates of the program are prepared to work in industrial defense corporations, hospitals, the aviation industry, emergency medical services, shopping mall security, regional security offices, public utility offices, and state and federal emergency management. Several area high schools have developed programs in criminal justice that allow students to earn college credit toward the FSC&TC homeland security program.

"We at FSC&TC believe we have areas of expertise that will help meet the local, state, and national needs for homeland security," said McCormick. "We believe our program will prepare students to enter the workforce in these critical areas in this crucial time for our country. This program is an excellent example of the mission of a community college—to be responsive to the needs of the community, business, and industry."

MONROE COMMUNITY COLLEGE, NEW YORK

Much like its counterparts in Ohio and West Virginia, Monroe Community College (MCC), in Rochester, New York, is building on programs already in place. It has created the Homeland Security Management Institute as a regional source for training of first responders and other professionals whose jobs may place them in a leadership role in public safety crises. The institute, which opened in 2004, is directed by Colonel John J. Perrone, Jr., an Army veteran and former major in the Monroe County Sheriff's Department. The institute has benefited from its relationship with the college's existing programs in law enforcement and firefighting. "This is a start-up year for us, but the institute is co-located with the Public Safety

Training Center," said Perrone. "As a whole, Monroe Community College has been in the business of training first responders in Monroe County for the past three decades. On an annual basis, we train over 5,000 first responders from 250 different agencies. The institute allows us to extend our reach to other first responders such as hospitals, utilities, private business, and public health. We already have trained hundreds in the first year."

Some of the institute's current offerings include community emergency response training for various community groups, risk and vulnerability programs, and weapons of mass destruction. There are two online training courses and the recently launched public health courses "Incident Command System for Public Health" and "What Is Public Health?" Although the courses are generally noncredit, Perrone said that in the fall of 2005, the institute would partner with the Law and Justice Academic Program at MCC's Damon Campus and would offer an associate degree in emergency management.

Perrone and other college officials have been seeking support for the institute by meeting with local law enforcement leaders and by soliciting state and federal funding. Senator Hillary Clinton (D-NY) visited the center and praised the college's efforts. Perrone hopes to expand the institute's offerings and believes that it might become a model for homeland security training across the nation. "Our future goals include expanding our training base to other disciplines as well as building on the college's capacity to offer distance learning," said Perrone. "Ultimately we'd like to be considered the training institute of choice on a regional and national level."

COMMUNITY COLLEGE OF ALLEGHENY COUNTY/CARNEGIE MELLON'S SOFTWARE ENGINEERING INSTITUTE

One program that has its origins as a national model is the cybersecurity training program at the Community College of Allegheny County (CCAC) in Pittsburgh, Pennsylvania. The college has joined forces with Carnegie Mellon University's Software Engineering Institute (SEI) to develop a cybersecurity curriculum that will serve as a standard for 2-year colleges across the country. The U.S. National Guard Bureau awarded the institutions $1.3 million to design courses that will help companies defend their computer systems and survive a cyberattack. The SIE has worldwide recognition for its efforts to develop security practices to protect systems against current and emerging threats. In collaboration with CCAC, the SEI has structured the 13-credit survivability and information certificate, which will arm network and system administrators with the necessary skill for recognizing, resisting, and recovering from attacks on network systems. Students enrolled in the hands-on program will have the opportunity to defend a network against simulated "cyberattacks." Community colleges that "partner" with CCAC to offer the certificate will deliver the course content and perform student assessment; however,

CCAC will maintain nationwide consistency by ensuring that those institutions have adequate facilities and certified instructors.

AMERICAN ASSOCIATION OF COMMUNITY COLLEGES AND LEAGUE FOR INNOVATION IN THE COMMUNITY COLLEGE

As community colleges move to the forefront on homeland security in their own regions, the American Association of Community Colleges (AACC) has begun coordinating efforts on a national scale. Last year, a 21-member task force was convened to define a long-range strategy for the nation's 1,175 two-year colleges. The AACC Ad Hoc Task Force on Homeland Security includes 18 community college presidents and 3 senior specialists at institutions with advanced programs and demonstrated expertise in defense and security. They hope to tap into the unique role of community colleges, which now educate more than 80% of the country's fire, police, and emergency medical personnel. At the local level, this means diversifying training such as port security in Miami and border security in southern Texas.

Likewise, the League for Innovation in the Community College has mounted a Homeland Security Initiative, calling 2-year colleges the "linchpin" in the fields of law enforcement and public safety. League members have held several summits on homeland security and the issues that are raised about this emerging field of education and training. While acknowledging that colleges are responding to the emergency preparedness needs evolving from terrorist actions and natural disasters that pose threats to communities, the league is urging its members to foresee the future of homeland security. Questions raised at summit discussions include the following:

- What will the homeland security workforce of the future look like?
- Will developing training programs clash with principles of civil liberties?
- Should preparing students to help their community in a time of crisis become part of general education initiatives? If so, does this mean that we must live in a state of constant readiness of attack?

As leaders of community colleges embrace an increasing role in homeland security, they also are pondering how to proceed over the longer term.

Note. From "Community Colleges in the Lead with Homeland Security," by M. Gilroy, 2005, *The Hispanic Outlook in Higher Education, 15*(12), p. 31. Copyright 1997–2004 by Hispanic Outlook. Adapted with permission.

CASE *12*

Community College, University, and Corporate Partnership to Combat Employment Shortages

Valerie J. Palamountain

Community-based campuses help employers overcome labor shortages. This case study describes such a program.

ecause of anticipated attrition and retirement, the Lockheed Martin operations plan forecasted a shortage of 6,500–11,000 information technology (IT) professionals over the next few years. The decrease in numbers in the available pool of IT professionals coupled with the increase in demand for professionals in science and engineering, encouraged Lockheed Martin to invest in local talent and to train students from area high schools in the Lockheed Martin operations and culture. Lockheed Martin Information Systems & Solutions (IS&S), located in King of Prussia, Pennsylvania, a suburb of Philadelphia, took bold action. Working with the School District of Philadelphia and the Philadelphia Youth Network (PYN), IS&S recruited promising high school juniors and seniors from the inner city and provided them with intensive training in IT.

The curriculum, developed by Bucks County Community College, Newtown, Pennsylvania, included both technical and workplace skills. The program was approved by the Pennsylvania Department of Labor and Industry as an IT registered apprenticeship. On graduation from high school, the apprentices had the opportunity to interview for permanent positions at Lockheed Martin and to continue their education at Bucks County Community College to earn an associate degree that articulated with a baccalaureate at Pennsylvania State University (PSU).

THE LARGER ENVIRONMENT

Lockheed Martin IS&S is a major government defense contractor with more than 3,000 employees in King of Prussia, Pennsylvania, and plans to expand. The need for IT professionals could be met by seeking personnel offshore or by developing talent from within. Lockheed Martin IS&S chose to develop internal talent through the apprenticeship program and thereby address numerous corporate objectives:

- Provide diversity in the Lockheed Martin workforce
- Recruit underrepresented populations in the IT profession
- Contribute to a healthy economy by investing in the domestic workforce
- Provide community service

Service to the community is a cornerstone of the Lockheed Martin values. The IT apprenticeship program offered the opportunity to serve the community, develop the skills of the individual employees, and promote the economic development of the region by retaining local jobs.

ACADEMIC PARTNERS

Bucks County Community College Center for Business & Industry Training (CBIT) developed the curriculum and provided the instructors for the program. CBIT was uniquely qualified to develop a program that met industry needs while providing the student support services required by high school juniors and seniors. The instructors selected for the program had extensive experience in the business environment and were able to relate to the needs of the students. Bucks County Community College is located in suburban Philadelphia and has a population of approximately 9,500 students. All courses, assessments, and testing were offered at IS&S during or at the end of the workday.

PSU became involved to meet the client's need for advanced degrees. PSU and Bucks County Community College worked together to develop a bidirectional articulation agreement. The apprentices could take courses simultaneously at both Bucks County Community College and PSU, working on an associate degree from the community college and a certificate program at PSU. The reciprocal agreement gave the apprentices the opportunity to work on multiple credentials simultaneously: Credits taken at Bucks County Community College could be applied toward the certificate program at PSU; credits taken at PSU could be applied toward the associate degree at Bucks County Community College. On completion of the associate degree, all credits were fully accepted by PSU toward a baccalaureate.

Other Players

The School District of Philadelphia identified four inner-city high schools that recommended the apprentices for the program. The Pennsylvania Department of Labor and Industry certified the IT apprenticeship program—the first registered program of its kind in Pennsylvania. The Philadelphia Youth Network (PYN) provided transportation from Philadelphia to Lockheed Martin in King of Prussia. Several agencies of the Commonwealth of Pennsylvania participated in planning the program: the Department of Education, the Bureau for Career and Technical Education Apprenticeship Program, and the Department of Labor Law and Compliance. IS&S participated in the formulation, planning, and execution of the IT apprenticeship program. Lockheed Martin personnel devoted their personal time and commitment as volunteer mentors to the apprentices.

The Problem

Lockheed Martin IS&S identified the need for a significant number of IT professionals to meet the anticipated need based on their contractual obligations. Attrition, retirement, and a shortage of professionals entering the profession contributed to the demand for IT professionals. There was a need to encourage youth to enter the profession and to enroll in a rigorous training program. In addition, IS&S had established goals to recruit underrepresented populations, specifically women and minorities, to the IT profession.

Jobs, workforce skills, quality, and workplace excellence were the goals of the program as stated by former Secretary of the Pennsylvania Department of Labor, Johnny Butler. To survive in a fiercely competitive environment, creative ideas to address labor shortages and skills gaps are necessary. The IT apprenticeship addresses a critical need for highly skilled workers with an innovative approach to attract underrepresented populations in a profession that offers career advancement.

Problem Analysis

The Lockheed Martin IS&S IT apprenticeship program is a collaborative effort of IS&S, the School District of Philadelphia, and PYN. The selection process required the involvement of both Lockheed Martin and the School District of Philadelphia to develop the selection criteria. Prospective apprentices were interviewed by a selection panel consisting of Lockheed Martin professionals. Contingency plans were made for students who declined or were unable to complete the IT apprenticeship program.

CBIT already provided customized job training to incumbent workers at Lockheed Martin. CBIT became involved with the IT apprenticeship program as the education provider, because of its success in customized job training for incumbent workers at Lockheed Martin. The original curriculum for the IT apprentices concentrated on developing technical skills. CBIT recognized the necessity of workplace readiness skills and incorporated training in essential business skills. The resulting curriculum is shown in Table 12.1.

Table 12.1	Technical and Workplace Readiness Skills Taught in the IS&S IT Apprenticeship Program	
Technical Skills	**Business and Interpersonal Skills**	
Microsoft Word proficiency	Time management	
Microsoft Excel proficiency	Résumé writing	
Microsoft Power Point proficiency	Business writing fundamentals	
Microsoft Office Web integration	Interpersonal communication	
Configuration Management (Clearcase)	Effective business communication	
UNIX (advanced topics for users)	Effective presentation	
Microsoft Project and Artemis	Teamwork	
HTML	Interviewing skills	
XML		
Unix Shell Programming (C Shell)		
DBMS Utilities and Tools (Oracle and Access)		
CGI scripting fundamentals		
Perl scripting fundamentals		
Adv C		
Adv C++		
JavaScript programming		
DHTML		
Excel macros with VBA		
Adv PC configuration and troubleshooting		
Oracle 8i (database administration)		

The training provided not only the technical skills needed but also the business and interpersonal skills that prepared the apprentices for the workplace. Remedial courses in English and math also were offered, as needed. In addition, Lockheed Martin educated the apprentices on business processes unique to the corporation. Also included in the apprenticeship were job shadowing, rotational assignments, hands-on training, and projects that used the skills the apprentices had acquired. The experiential learning gave the apprentices the opportunity to accomplish work assignments in a business environment and to identify the career track that best suited their individual talents.

PSU and Bucks County Community College worked together to develop a curriculum that was acceptable to both institutions and that met the needs of the business partner. To encourage the apprentices to continue their education, Lockheed Martin IS&S initiated discussions between PSU and Bucks County Community College to develop an articulation agreement providing the apprentices with a certificate from PSU in information systems technology, which included courses offered by Bucks County Community College; an Associate's degree in IT from Bucks County Community College, which included courses offered by PSU; and a baccalaureate in IT from PSU with full articulation with the Bucks County Community College AAS degree. The apprentices have the option to complete any phase or complete the entire educational program. Working together, Bucks County Community College and PSU agreed to accept the credits of both institutions in a reciprocal arrangement. The goals of both institutions were to assist the apprentices in completing the highest level of education possible for each of them. In many cases, the apprentices were the first in their families to enter college.

Recognizing that the apprentices would require additional support, Lockheed Martin IS&S asked employees to act as mentors. The mentors offered guidance and the voice of experience to familiarize the apprentices in areas such as employee benefits, to provide advice on setting educational and career goals, and to assist the students in their high school studies. The employee mentors were a key component in the success of the program. Assessment testing was conducted during the workday for all of the apprentices interested in entering college. Remedial classes and college-level courses were offered on site at Lockheed Martin IS&S immediately after the end of the workday to encourage the apprentices to continue their education. College courses were reimbursed through the tuition reimbursement benefit offered by IS&S. Involving the parents and guardians of the apprentices was also critical to the success of the program. Every effort was made to keep the parents and guardians informed about the progress of the apprentices and to include them in celebrations of achievement.

LESSONS LEARNED

The planning portion of the IT apprenticeship program focused on recruiting high school students. Recruiting high school students required the involvement of human resources because of the age of the students. Initially, little consideration was given to the social and business skills that the apprentices would need. During the first few months, IS&S recognized that the apprentices lacked the business and social skills to fit into the organization. The focus shifted from technical skills training to interpersonal, business, and communications skills. An internal marketing plan was necessary to have the program accepted throughout the organization.

Assistance to the program was necessary for the apprentices to gain the full benefit of the mentorship and experiential learning opportunities. Personal counseling for the individual apprentices was necessary to understand the magnitude of the opportunity available to them. A case manager would have benefited the program and possibly prevented inappropriate behaviors in the apprentices.

RESULTS

The IT apprenticeship is a 3-year program. During their junior year, the apprentices attended their high school classes 4 days per week, and spent 1 day each week in training at Lockheed Martin IS&S. During the summer between junior and senior years, the apprentices were employed by IS&S and continued their training. In their senior year, the apprentices spent 3 days in class at their high schools and 2 days in training at IS&S. Upon graduation from high school, the apprentices continued training and had the opportunity to interview for permanent positions within Lockheed Martin. At the conclusion of the 3 years, 20 of the apprentices in the first cohort graduated from high school, completed the apprenticeship training, were working full time at Lockheed Martin, and had entered college. By September 2004, two additional cohorts of 20 to 22 apprentices each had started at IS&S in King of Prussia, and a cohort of 12 apprentices had started at the Lockheed Martin site in Arizona.

One of the objectives of the IT apprenticeship program was to provide a means to involve the Lockheed Martin IS&S in the development of the high school curriculum. After the initial year of the program, the IT apprenticeship was recognized as a corporate best practice. Plans were made to expand it to additional Lockheed Martin sites in Arizona, Colorado, and the District of Columbia. The expansion program targeted additional underserved populations, specifically, Hispanics and Native Americans.

PART 3

Case Studies of Community Colleges Helping Students With Career Development

In a dynamic post-industrial economy, people need help to transition not just from one job to another but sometimes from one career to another. Community colleges play a role in helping individuals qualify for career transitions, illustrated in the following cases.

Case 13. The Career Pathways Initiative at Elizabethtown Community and Technical College

Case 14. The Career Pathways Initiative at Gateway Community and Technical College

Case 15. The Career Pathways Initiative at Owensboro Community and Technical College

Case 16. Brownfields Training Program Readies Environmental Workers in North Carolina

Case 17. Encouraging Careers in Manufacturing

Case 18. Economic Development Office Provides Career Development to Entrepreneurs in Virginia

CASE *13*

The Career Pathways Initiative at Elizabethtown Community and Technical College

Keith Bird

Community colleges do more than meet employer needs. They also meet the needs of individuals to keep up with dynamic labor markets. This case study documents one such program, as do Cases 14 and 15.

The Kentucky Community and Technical College System (KCTCS) Career Pathways project is a statewide initiative that is being implemented in each of KCTCS's 16 college districts, with policy guidance and technical assistance provided by system staff in the chancellor's office. KCTCS defines a career pathway as a series of connected educational programs, with integrated work experience and support services that enable students to combine school and work and advance over time to better jobs and higher levels of education and training. Career pathways are targeted to regional labor markets, focused on employment sectors, and provide a framework for workforce development by integrating the programs and resources of community colleges and other education providers, workforce agencies, and social service providers. It is important to note that a career pathway is not a program per se but rather a systemic framework for a new way of doing business in our colleges and communities. The ultimate goal is for the pathway to provide a seamless system of career exploration and preparation with multiple entry and exit points that spans elementary, secondary, and postsecondary education.

ORIGIN OF CAREER PATHWAYS AT KCTCS

Three factors converged to lead KCTCS to identify career pathways as an effective mechanism and policy lever to transform the way that its institutions do business and respond to the needs of both students and business. First, KCTCS wanted a systemic framework to better support the workforce development needs of regional and statewide industry clusters. KCTCS wanted to move from providing customized training on a business-by-business basis to a more strategic workforce development approach to better anticipate the current and future needs of industry clusters that are important to regional labor markets. Second, KCTCS was committed to providing multiple education pathways for students and workers that were easily accessed and provided opportunities for upward mobility in their careers. These multiple pathways would build on the best practices identified by the tech prep movement and provide smooth transitions from secondary to 4-year institutions. The final factor leading to developing this Career Pathways initiative was KCTCS's Bridges to Opportunity planning grant from the Ford Foundation. Ford's hypothesis is that community colleges will increase access and success for low-income adults through improved integration of the three primary missions: academic, workforce development, and remediation (student services).

KCTCS was created in 1997 by the Kentucky Postsecondary Education Improvement Act to improve the quality of life of Kentuckians by expanding opportunities provided by the state's 2-year public colleges. KCTCS consolidated 28 community and technical colleges into 16 districts with 65 campuses. This seamless system of higher education allows students to move easily among programs and institutions as they pursue academic and technical degrees and workforce training. KCTCS is making higher education more accessible, more relevant, and more responsive to the needs of citizens, employers, and communities, with a goal of doubling its enrollment by the year 2020. In fall 2004, 81,990 credit students were enrolled at KCTCS—58% were part-time students, and 42% were full-time students. In addition, 14,297 high school students were enrolled (dual credit) in 2003–2004. Further, 38,000 students enrolled in distance learning and Web-assisted courses. In 2003–2004, 12,740 credentials were granted: 4,764 associate degrees, 2,226 diplomas, and 5,750 certificates.

The Career Pathways initiative has been implemented in each of the 16 KCTCS districts; with 12 in the health-care industry, 3 in manufacturing, and 1 in construction trades. Programs at Gateway Community and Technical College and Owensboro Community and Technical College are described in Cases 14 and 15. The program at Elizabethtown Community and Technical College (ECTC) is described here.

For more than 40 years, ECTC has been serving residents of rural south central Kentucky. The service area encompasses 11 counties where 38% of working-age adults are at literacy levels 1 and 2, and 70 % of incoming freshmen are required to enroll in one or more developmental courses. Notably, the region's culture of low educational attainment is further illustrated by census data indicating that less than 7.8% of the adult residents possess a bachelor's degree. The college serves a rapidly changing student body, which is composed of 5,000 students, the majority of whom are under- or unemployed, many receiving aid through the Workforce Investment Act as well as through traditional financial aid sources. The institution is Title III designated by the U.S. Department of Education.

Several factors made a significant difference in the college's ability to develop fully integrated planning and support in the community of the local career pathways program concepts. First is the export of over 4,000 well-paid manufacturing sector jobs overseas. Many of these residents had been removed from the formal educational systems for over 20 years. This loss profoundly affected schools, health facilities, and government and service sectors. The predominantly White students are commuters from insulated rural areas, but the fastest-growing population of students are minorities and nontraditional aged students.

THE PATHWAY INITIATIVE AT ECTC

The NorthStar Healthcare Initiative, led by ECTC, is a demand-driven, replicable, and sustainable career system model. The model was based on regional strategic planning involving the education, business and industry, and government and service sectors. The model is based on the following principles:

- The delivery of just-in-time education modules and programs plus support services to address short- and long-term gaps in the workforce systems.
- A commitment to base course development and program expansion decisions on employment projections of need defined by future technology, local demographics, retirements, and projected industry expansion.
- The initiative required the partners to inventory resources and services and examine how collectively the region might reallocate resources to achieve goals through the reduction of cross-sector duplication.

The primary components of pathway services include the following: (1) installation of a one-stop health career and education center located in a hospital to gain access to a broad section of the community and (2) the creation of short-term rapidly deployable education courses as defined by industry surveys to aid immediate needs for training. Examples include "Spanish for Healthcare Workers," fast-track medical terminology courses, security officer training, and career orientation courses for targeted high-need careers such as respiratory therapy, radiography, nursing, and clinical laboratory assisting. In addition, the model includes expansion of COMPASS testing centers throughout the region in the adult education centers with specialized advisement for health careers. Youth programs and a unified referral system between the partners were other critical elements. After a full year of planning and a full year of preliminary implementation to work out system glitches, the program was fully implemented in the third year, with plans for a first replication to begin prior to the year end.

The planning for the Career Pathways initiative included a cross-section of 63 partners, which were surveyed to identify current, short-term, and long-term workplace shortages. The region's second largest employer with more than 2,000 employees, Hardin Memorial Hospital, became the lead representative for the health-care sector, the college for the educational sector, and the Workforce Investment Board (WIB) for the employment and government services sector. These lead partners formed a governing board to facilitate model development and deployment. The concept of the model was to use the large health-care employers scattered throughout the region to develop and deliver new education components becoming mirror images of one another in providing new levels of services to both incumbent workers and their communities. The first stage of development occurred at Hardin Memorial Hospital.

THE PARTNERSHIP

At the system level, the Ford Bridges to Opportunities State Team included senior policymakers from Adult Education, the Kentucky WIB, and the Kentucky Cabinet for Health and Family Services. These partners participated in technical assistance sessions from the Ford Foundation and encouraged their local constituents to participate in Career Pathways at the local level. Through community development activities, ECTC engaged partners in a new manner for the institution. The first step was to survey a cross-section and meet with health-care industry providers from the following disciplines and groups: acute and long-term care, transitional and assisted living facilities, district health departments, services providers for the aging, physicians groups, home care providers, and education providers. The college also worked with the local P–16 Council, WIB and its partner agencies, and local economic development authorities and chambers of commerce. This level of participation has allowed the project to attract $200,000 in grants, plus an estimated $500,000 in local contributions to date.

The hospitals provided commercial space and staff support for the Career and Education Center, creation and renovation of a clinical laboratory and equipment for a new respiratory therapy program, and support of a faculty salary buy-down program to allow access to industry practicing professionals in high-need health-care fields (through short-term cross-posting of positions while maintaining full pay and benefits to meet industry standards). The hospitals leveraged public relations contracts, allowing reduced cost-sharing for the development of marketing materials, purchase of air time, and development of commercials and video testimonials to be used across the region.

The WIB provided staffing to support the career center, strategic planning leadership support through speakers, two fully mobile wireless classrooms to allow the partners to work together for job fairs, and recruitment events for practitioners to take advantage of teachable moments throughout clinical settings. The WIB further assisted through the purchase of marketing materials, purchase of health library books and materials to support new health-care programs, student equipment and scholarships, and staff to support and manage the career center and referral processes. The college provided staffing for coordination of all programs, course development, allocation of a new ITV room and ITV mobile unit to expand its ability to deliver courses from any location to the students. The integration and use of v-brick technology allowed the expansion of options for simulcasting of training as well.

NINE KEY PRINCIPLES

1. Career Pathways Is a Systemic Framework

It is important to understand that adding an allied health program or two for a health-care pathway is only a part of developing a career pathway. A pathway must include a variety of other components that are responsive to the needs of an industry sector, its incumbent workers, and emerging workers. The Career Pathways initiative requires that colleges identify the current and future needs of an industry sector or cluster, and then provide a series of connected educational programs, with integrated work experience and support services that enable students to combine school and work and advance over time to better jobs and higher levels of education and training. Career pathways provide a framework for workforce development by integrating the programs and resources of community colleges and other education providers, workforce agencies, and social service providers. An effective Career Pathways model incorporates a targeted remedial bridge as well as a carefully negotiated articulation agreement with the relevant 4-year institutions.

2. Career Pathways Are a Strategic Tool for Institutional Transformation

The development of career pathways requires mission integration, whereby the academic, student, and workforce sides of the community college work closely together to develop the connected educational programs. Academic faculty and department chairs have an opportunity to better understand the needs of business and industry as they interact with business partners in a way not previously done. A Career Pathways model also forces colleges to transform to accommodate employer and incumbent worker needs by developing curriculum in alternative formats (modularization), delivering courses at alternative times (evening and weekend programs) and at alternative sites (on site at hospitals and job sites), and providing intensive career counseling and advising and other support services in a case management format. Additionally, career pathways present an opportunity to make stronger connections with sending high schools to reduce the need for remediation at the postsecondary level.

3. Career Pathways Are Policy and Funding Levers

Career pathways are strong levers to identify and implement policy and funding changes that enhance the responsiveness of community colleges to businesses and students. In Kentucky these policies have included business and industry training credit: academic credit for workplace learning, fractional credit, quick turnaround on developing new courses (certificate approval), open-entry and open-exit programming (modularizing curriculum), and the development of tuition-based modularized academic credit courses that provide easier access to Pell grants and other forms of student aid. On the funding front, career pathways require the leveraging of a variety of funding sources. In Kentucky these funds have included Kentucky WINS (use of Workforce Development Trust Funds for credit and credential based education/training); Workforce Investment Act funds; Workforce Alliance, including Adult Education funds; and industry contributions (i.e., employer tuition reimbursement dollars, visiting faculty, equipment donations, and internships).

4. Career Pathways Are a Transition Tool From Secondary to Postsecondary Education and Beyond

Career pathways provide a framework for formalizing and specifying many of the articulation and transfer agreements between secondary, postsecondary, adult education, and the workplace. Pathways present a myriad of transition possibilities well beyond the traditional 4 (secondary) +2 (community college) +2 (baccalaureate). We must now think of multiple pathways across a life of continuous learning. Pathways systems also strengthen the message that all incumbent and emerging workers will need some postsecondary education if they want to earn a living wage in the 21st century and, in fact, provide the access points for both the traditional and nontraditional students. Career pathways support and encourage transition programs such as Early Middle College, dual enrollment and credit programs with secondary as well as adult basic education, and ESL or remedial bridge programs.

5. Career Pathways Are an Economic Development Tool

With the globalization of the workforce, intellectual talent can be found almost anywhere on earth. Any work that can be digitized can be done anywhere. Extensive research and literature suggest that communities, regions, and states will be most competitive if they support and grow industry clusters that are important to their region. One critical component of this support is the growth of human capital. Since career pathways are focused around regional or statewide industry sectors and not a single business, the development of pathways provides a strong strategic advantage in supplying the talent needed by the growing clusters. Pathways also focus on all aspects of the workforce needs—from entry level technicians to PhD-level scientists and engineers. In Kentucky there are several clusters that have been identified for either current or future career pathway development: health care, automotive/advanced manufacturing, equine, coal and energy, and bio-life sciences.

6. Career Pathways Are a Tool to Strengthen and Formalize Connections to Business

Effective career pathways must be demand-driven: They must meet the current and future needs of businesses. Career pathways are sometimes called career ladder or lattice initiatives or industry-focused advancement initiatives. But whatever the name, they must meet the needs of industry sectors. Since pathways require that strong relationships be developed and continuously nurtured with businesses, community colleges and their partners can be more responsive to ongoing changes in workforce needs because of the strength of the existing relationships and a more in-depth knowledge of the industry. In Kentucky there is another initiative that is closely aligned with this aspect of career pathways, the "Certified Workforce," which uses the Kentucky Manufacturing Skills Standards, the Kentucky Employability Certificate, and other industry-based credentials to certify certain skills to employers.

7. Career Pathways Are a Tool to Enhance Community Strategic Partnerships

Career pathways cannot be developed in a vacuum. It is critical that multiple partners be fully engaged in the process: the academic side of the community college (including remedial education), the workplace/continuing education side of the community college, business and industry, WIBs and their One-Stop partners, secondary education (both technical and academic), adult basic education, and 4-year institutions (public and private). Often community colleges are well positioned to play the role of intermediary in these efforts, but it is important to determine case by case who is the best partner to play the intermediary role in a specific community. This intermediary role is one of a convener, facilitator, and resource coordinator who ensures that all partners are at the table.

8. Career Pathways Are an Upward Mobility Tool

One of the key goals of the Career Pathways initiative is to provide students and workers with a clear map to navigate their course to better jobs and wealth creation for themselves and their families. Career pathways often provide an opportunity for people to integrate work and school, rather than having to choose one or the other. The pathways provide a better understanding of the way labor markets work by developing career maps that have both lateral and vertical movement. Most workers cannot afford to give up their earnings to return to school full time, so career pathways provide a structured framework for advancing careers through a combination of multiple training delivery modes such as work-based and campus-based training, part-time courses, and Web-based courses. Additionally, many students (at both the secondary and postsecondary level) can greatly benefit from some type of applied, work-based learning (i.e., internships and apprenticeships).

9. Career Pathways Are an Accountability Tool

Historically, community colleges have often used anecdotal information to "tell their story" rather than focusing on data-driven decision making and accountability. This trend is beginning to change, and career pathways provide an excellent framework for this transition. The Ford and Lumina Foundations have partnered to engage the 10 states participating in Ford's Bridges to Opportunity and Lumina's Achieving the Dream initiatives in a data collections and analysis project. This joint effort aims to improve the use of state data in state strategies to increase access and attainment of underserved community and technical college students. Additionally, the Perkins Act, which has suffered from questionable or incomplete data, is up for reauthorization. A career pathways system and its accompanying data and outcomes present substantial opportunity for enhanced accountability under Perkins. Kentucky is also under discussions to join the College and Career Transitions Initiative sponsored by the League for Innovation in the Community College, which supports and requires accountability.

At ECTC, the Career Pathways initiative has provided a new framework for how the community college conducts business internally as well as with their community partners. KCTCS assists by measuring the success of individual students in programs, support services, and employment outcomes. Perhaps more importantly, the Career Pathways model will provide this institution with a strategy and tools to maximize its ability to support industry needs and projections. Another important aspect of the process is the tracking of cohort groups of students as they transition through the P–16 system to the workplace

ECTC's Health-Care Training Challenge

ECTC's primary challenge was to develop its role in assisting the region in economic recovery and transition and to address the export of the manufacturing sector. Addressing the underprepared workforce and supporting the rapid growth within the health-care system emerged as critically important. The community partners realized that economic development and educational institutions operating within their respective silos was a liability and did not support the necessary infrastructure for meeting the identified community needs. With no real solutions apparent, the community embarked on development of a holistic system to address its barriers to economic growth, which resulted in a health-care approach.

ECTC and its partners examined the health-care data on employers, employment trends, services, and local demographics through use of census data, Kentucky health-care system reports, and Department of Labor wage and salary data and forecasts. Additionally, ECTC surveyed 53 employers representing nearly 1,000 incumbent workers within the health-care system prior to developing solutions and priorities. The partners also examined adult and family literacy issues and transition issues between educational components and examined whether the local business practices of partner agencies and providers were truly serving clients in the most effective and efficient manner.

In order to solve the critical shortage of respiratory care practitioners due to impending retirements and high industry need, ECTC created a satellite program through an accredited neighboring KCTCS community college with a strong program. The partners projected the need and decided prior to implementation how many class cycles would be needed to address the shortage. After addressing the respiratory care shortage with two training cycles, the partners plan to convert resources to a new program such as certified medical assisting. The concept is to fill needs and stop local brain drain by converting programs to fit local needs. Another strategy was to increase awareness of alternative health careers through sophisticated marketing of alternative programs and increased training and testing sites to assist low wage workers in accessing the system by obtaining basic and core courses that will allow them to enter advanced education programs.

While the KCTCS pathways are currently under development or in early implementation stages, the chancellor's office has developed a two-pronged approach to measuring accountability and outcomes. In its broadest sense, a career pathways strategy requires a systemic transformation that should be reflected in the overall program statistics. Therefore, at the system level, KCTCS will track all students enrolled in the program area addressed by the career pathway (i.e., nursing, manufacturing, construction, etc.). This will allow KCTCS to compare the comprehensive impact of the career pathways strategy with previous program performance at that institution and the pathway program's performance with the same program's performance at another institution without a pathway strategy for that career sector. Performance indicators will include number of dual-enrollment students, percentages enrolled in developmental education, developmental education success rates (percentage passing the first entry-level course), GPAs, the number of transfers to programs outside the pathway, credits earned per semester, credits earned at separation, credentials earned, and numbers of students transferring to 4-year institutions.

The second prong of the accountability process will track individual student outcomes for those students who receive resources or services through the Pathways strategy that would not otherwise be available to them. Each college will flag individual Pathways students meeting this definition of services, which will allow the chancellor's office to extract performance information for this targeted group of students from a wealth of performance data in the existing student data system.

In addition, colleges will be responsible for gathering and reporting aggregate information regarding participation in events or services that involve non–KCTCS participants (promoting pathways to K–12 audiences, adult basic education audiences, etc.). Interim program results for the NorthStar Career Pathway system in the first year include services to more than 2,300 clients. ECTC developed and deployed five new courses, implemented one new degree program (respiratory care), and connected at a new operational level with more than 63 partners, creating a foundation for the future stability of the processes through shared governance.

LESSONS LEARNED

KCTCS colleges are finding the Career Pathways initiative to be a unique tool that enables them to meet previously identified and longstanding workforce development needs within their individual communities with a more comprehensive and long-term approach than has previously existed. With a KCTCS commitment of $3.6 million in seed funding for 16 Career Pathway grants, the colleges have leveraged over $3 million in cash and in-kind support from employers and other community partners to serve a projected 2,500 students (incumbent and emerging employees) over a 2-year period.

At the system level, KCTCS has learned that the development of a comprehensive career pathway is as much about the process as the product. It takes both time and patience as the colleges work to integrate themselves internally (academic, workforce development, remediation, and student support missions). The colleges are reinventing themselves in order to better meet the needs of their students and the demands of business and industry. The development of a career pathway ensures a continuous feedback loop that will fuel an ongoing continuous improvement relationship between the college and employment sector and the community partners that have been engaged.

Lessons learned at ECTC include the critical need to provide advancement options for underemployed, unemployed, and low-wage workers. The regional health-care system was a very different type of employer than the traditional manufacturing sector employer. The hospitals typically promoted from within and had less than a 5% employee turnover. Thus, if there were not programs to assist the incumbent workers first, the creation of opportunities for emerging and underemployed workers to advance was impossible.

Another important lesson was that just-in-time delivery of programs such as respiratory therapy could be creatively accomplished in under 6 months from intake and orientation to start of classes. Partnerships with a strong accredited program within the KCTCS system through a shared funding agreement and use of existing approved curriculum were contributing factors. The health-care industry is providing guarantees for filling new classes for the length of the program, in addition to clinical sites and laboratories.

While shared governance is difficult, partnerships are what allows the rapid progress to implementation and the attraction of resources. Getting past the individual operational silos is the biggest ongoing battle, which has partially been diffused by shared decision making and agreement for operation of the project under a unified identity whereby all partners receive the same amount of acknowledgment for success. Thus, the use of NorthStar as the pathways identity and the independent board circumvented many turf issues and refocused the partners on what is best for the community.

CASE 14

The Career Pathways Initiative at Gateway Community and Technical College

Keith Bird

Community colleges do more than meet employer needs. They also meet the needs of individuals to keep up with dynamic labor markets. This case study documents one such program, as do Cases 13 and 15.

Gateway Community and Technical College (GCTC) is part of a statewide system of 2-year public community and technical colleges created by the Postsecondary Education Improvement Act of 1997. This Act consolidated Kentucky's community colleges and postsecondary technical schools within a new organization, the Kentucky Community and Technical College System (KCTCS). In 2002, three northern Kentucky postsecondary technical schools became GCTC. The region had been without a comprehensive community college since 1968, when Northern Kentucky Community College ended its community college mission and transformed into Northern Kentucky University, a 4-year institution with a current enrollment of 14,000 students.

GCTC serves the northern region of Kentucky that borders Indiana and Ohio and is an integral part of the Cincinnati Primary Metropolitan Statistical Area, with a population of 2 million. The college awards certificates, diplomas, and associate degrees in art, science, and applied sciences in over 40 programs of study in business and information technology, allied health, industrial and transportation technologies, early childhood education, and arts and sciences. The Business and Industry Services Division provides hundreds of workforce development classes annually at the workplace, in the community, and on campus. GCTC, one of the fastest-growing institutions within KCTCS, enrolled 1,000 students in 2000–2001. Spring 2005 headcount enrollment surpassed 3,000 and is anticipated to reach 5,000 by the 2006–2007 academic year.

Demographic data collected on the students enrolling in Spring 2005 indicates the following:

- 44% women; 56% men
- 76% part time; 24% full time
- Average age, 27
- 93% White, non-Hispanic
- 4% African American, non-Hispanic
- 1% American Indian, Alaskan Native, Asian, or Pacific Islander
- 1% Hispanic
- 33% received need-based financial assistance
- 75% were first-generation college students

GCTC's Pathway Initiative

The manufacturing career pathway at GCTC links associate degree, diploma, and certificate programs in manufacturing disciplines to manufacturing job placement in the Northern Kentucky area. The pathway's goal is to articulate a roadmap for people who want to build a career in manufacturing. The pathway clearly communicates how different levels of educational credentials relate to job titles and compensation. The intent is to enable people to make informed decisions about education based on a realistic appraisal of the job market. The pathway is currently targeting juniors and seniors in high school, incumbent workers, dislocated workers, One Stop clients and adult education students.

On the education side of the pathway, GCTC's initiative has focused on linking the college's manufacturing programs vertically from secondary schools to 4-year institutions. On the industry side of the pathway, the initiative has sought employer requirements to drive the development of education programs. The key program to establish a complete pathway is the applied science degree in manufacturing engineering technology, which serves as a link between an associate degree at GCTC and earning a bachelor of science degree at the local 4-year institution.

The manufacturing career pathway serves manufacturers in the eight-county area of Northern Kentucky. These manufacturers range from small local businesses to Global 500 companies. They practice a wide range of manufacturing processes from discrete job shop machining to repetitive assembly operations. Their needs follow the national need for technically skilled employees who can work collaboratively to solve problems; who possess a broad understanding of manufacturing at the business, process, and technical levels; and who can couple that knowledge with the interpersonal and team skills needed to work with others to accomplish assigned projects. GCTC's pathway project has engaged community organizations in developing and communicating the pathway to potential participants. The Northern Kentucky Council of Partners in Education K–16, Northern Kentucky One Stop, and the Workforce Investment Board have participated in partner meetings that provide guidance to the pathway.

GCTC's project follows the principles described at the system level. Three principles stand out as key areas of focus. First is the principle that career pathways are a transition tool from secondary to postsecondary to lifelong learning. GCTC's manufacturing careers pathway encourages lifelong learning by offering numerous exit and entry points for those participants who move between the education and industry sides of the pathway. Second, GCTC's Career Pathways initiative is working to support informed decisions about careers for individuals and to build accountability for pathway outcomes. Finally, GCTC's career pathway is beginning to serve as a strategic tool for institutional transformation. Career pathways require integration across curricula, programs, and departments. At GCTC, the pathway is supporting other efforts to build integrated manufacturing programs. Participants in integrated manufacturing will gain knowledge and skills across disciplines and provide more value to employers.

GCTC's CHALLENGE

GCTC's career pathway project is not directed toward the needs of one employer. The pathway is driven by the need of manufacturers across Northern Kentucky to hire more technically qualified workers or to upgrade the technical knowledge and skills of their current workforce. Across the United States, manufacturing is undergoing a dramatic change. Much of the business press has emphasized the transfer of low-skilled manufacturing jobs to other parts of the world with lower wage scales, with the prognosis that these jobs are not likely to come back.

Manufacturers have responded by emphasizing cost reductions and greater innovation. Both of these initiatives have placed greater demands on the traditional manufacturing workforce. On the shop floor, computer skills, teamwork, and technical skills are in demand. The consensus is that that manufacturing is growing more technical as the workforce is growing less technical. The demand is for educated workers who possess a breadth of technical knowledge as well as the ability to work with others to accomplish goals. Increasingly, manufacturers are seeking employees with at least an associate degree.

To clearly define employer needs, GCTC conducted a survey and interviews with 17 manufacturers in Northern Kentucky. The survey participants were asked to rank order the most important entry-level knowledge and skills. In interviews, the employers were asked to explain their rankings and further define why they ranked items as important. The eight highest-ranked skills indicated by the surveys and interviews were as follows:

- Interpersonal skills
- Strong math skills
- Communication skills (speaking, presenting, and writing)
- Project management
- Teamwork
- Business-level understanding of manufacturing along with some understanding of manufacturing process and production operations
- Introductory CAD/CAM
- Quality control

GCTC's new associate of applied science in manufacturing engineering technology is built to address the needs cited by employers. Associated certificates have already been approved to provide the exit and entry points between the education and job sides of the pathway. The integrated manufacturing technologies certificate focuses on the technical skills used across manufacturing disciplines. The manufacturing operations certificate provides the business and process understanding required to solve cross-functional problems in manufacturing companies. Finally, the quality control certificate focuses on the technical skills required to maintain quality in manufacturing.

GCTC's manufacturing career pathway is at the beginning of gathering baseline data to evaluate its progress. In doing so, the pathway has initiated new discussions at the college about data accuracy. These conversations are going to add value as the pathway will begin to use data to evaluate outcomes rather than anecdotal evidence.

GCTC believes that the three new certificates will be the ticket to helping employees see the significance and immediate application of postsecondary learning. Experience has indicated that most employees who are mandated to take training have a somewhat pessimistic view of how they will use what they learn. Since they are leaning on old paradigms concerning learning, it makes sense that they are not expecting immediate application of classroom learning. The certificates are an excellent example of how students can learn something one evening and apply it the next day.

LESSONS LEARNED

To date, GCTC's pathway effort shows great promise. Employers have been supportive in a numbers of ways. They have participated in a survey and interviews, attended an initial meeting for employers, provided letters of support to obtain program approval for the AAS in manufacturing engineering technology, and volunteered to host high school students on plant tours to educate them about manufacturing. Secondary schools and community organizations are also engaged in and excited about the opportunity to improve results for students after secondary school. Two lessons learned stand out.

The first is that it is critical to have employers at the table from the beginning and for each subsequent discussion, making them instrumental in all decisions. Before the pathway was established, employers, secondary school administrators and teachers, and GCTC administrators and faculty provided valuable insight into how the pathway should look. In developing the AAS degree, all constituents provided their perspectives on what would be required to achieve a meaningful degree program. In this regard, employer feedback was important. It was, however, integrated with academic requirements to achieve a degree program that met employer needs on the industry side of the pathway while meeting the academic requirements on the education side of the pathway.

This was accomplished by listening to others and acting upon that feedback. For example, the development of the certificates was driven by employers who gave feedback that the pathway lacked exit and entry points. They also wanted credentials short of an associate degree. At the same time, any credentials had to meet academic requirements to fit into the pathway. The results were certificates that offer meaningful credentials while also requiring college-level math.

The second lesson learned is to provide value. This is particularly true for employers. When launching GCTC's pathway, the message to employers was that the pathway would prove valuable to them by providing technically skilled employees. Employers were not asked to sign up to be on a committee or to commit resources. All communication to employers is directed at what the value is to them and how their actions directly relate to gaining that value. For example, companies were sought to provide plant tours for high school students. The communication was that employers needed to volunteer to build a pipeline of students interested in manufacturing so that they will have technically skilled employees in the future. It was not sold as a "nice thing to do" but as an action that is directly related to their success. Although not everyone volunteered, three employers stepped forward to help. The clearer the value is to employers, the better.

In total, the impact of constant communication about how you are providing value while listening and taking action on that feedback is critically important. Communicating a clear value equation to employers is equally important and challenging. Together they will increase the chances of gaining buy-in and creating success for any pathways effort.

CASE *15*

The Career Pathways Initiative at Owensboro Community and Technical College

Keith Bird

Community colleges do more than meet employer needs. They also meet the needs of individuals to keep up with dynamic labor markets. This case study documents one such program, as do Cases 13 and 14.

Owensboro Community and Technical College (OCTC) is located in Owensboro, Kentucky, the industrial and cultural hub of western Kentucky and the third largest city in terms of population in the Commonwealth of Kentucky. Serving approximately 5,000 students per semester, OCTC is the primary provider of postsecondary education, workforce training, and lifelong learning opportunities for more than 140,000 citizens in Daviess, Hancock, Ohio, and McLean counties. On its three campuses, a comprehensive curriculum for technical and career programs leads to certificates, diplomas, and associate degrees preparing graduates for employment.

As a result of initiatives to improve the college-going rate in the region, OCTC recently ranked fourth in the nation in increased enrollment for colleges of its size. OCTC's highly acclaimed Discover College allows students to earn college credit while attending high school and its SkillTrain Center is having significant success in improving literacy for underprepared adults in the region. Using WorkKeys and the Kentucky Employability Certificate, over 4,000 potential employees for the local workforce have been assessed to date and have the opportunity to upgrade their skills at no cost through the SkillTrain Center.

OCTC's Pathways Inititative

OCTC's Advanced Manufacturing for the 21st Century career pathways model is a comprehensive, multi-phased approach that offers individuals a career pathway leading to employment or advancement through certifiable skill enhancement in the field of industrial maintenance. It uses WorkKeys assessments and profiling to identify the foundational skills present in entry-level manufacturing positions. Individuals are assessed with WorkKeys and are required to earn a Kentucky Employability Certificate as the first step in the pathway to continued learning. Postsecondary curriculum in the area of industrial maintenance has been enhanced to increase access and flexibility of delivery. The pathway offers an open-entry, open-exit educational format, accelerated academic programs and interactive and hands-on learning opportunities.

Industry partners seek to utilize the career pathway for hiring and incumbent worker skill enhancement, to develop and participate in collaboratively developed technical training programs, and to recognize project credentials in employment and promotion practices. Primary partners include local manufacturing companies such as DANA Corporation, Weyerhaeuser, Aleris, Century Aluminum, Kimberly Clark, and Unilever. Local community service agencies—the Department for Employment Services, the Green River Area Development District, the Owensboro One-Stop and other agency members—have provided employability skills training, job search assistance, referral services, counseling, transportation, child care, and other important assistance related to eliminating barriers to participation.

Seeking to differentiate Owensboro from other communities, policymakers set an ambitious economic development strategy to develop a better-trained, more competitive workforce. Armed with that high-stakes charge, OCTC reorganized outreach efforts under the auspices of its Center for Community and Economic Development (CCED), a cost-recovery division well versed in balancing service missions with financially stable market-driven activities. As a cross-functional team, CCED's goal is to maximize personnel and services while precluding "silo think." With more than 30 staff professionals and a dean of economic and workforce development, it is considered KCTCS's most comprehensive unit. A full range of adult education services, customized training, assessment services, continuing education and regulatory training, and special initiatives are offered. Participants—unemployed, underemployed, or incumbent workers—enter from multiple entry and delivery points. Its SkillTrain Center, a primary service location, prepares individuals for work or college with a host of open-entry services including free instruction and assessment in the WorkKeys areas commonly required for employment (reading, applied math, and locating information).

OCTC's Challenge

Many entry-level or small scale companies (defined as organizations with minimum skill requirements, lower wages, or smaller workforces) in the area were in crisis. Unlike their more profitable corporate neighbors, smaller-scale companies often lack the strategic vision or resources necessary to invest in their human capital. Workforce training seldom goes beyond the minimum requirements of on-the-job training or federally mandated safety training. With lack of opportunity for advancement and better wages, turnover rates are high. The tremendous costs associated with a revolving-door workforce often result in production delays, quality issues, and even layoffs when the organization cannot remain stable.

In addition, at-risk individuals seeking advanced career opportunities are often unaware of those available to them or lack the skills necessary to pursue such further education. More still lack the skills necessary to obtain or retain employment. Furthermore, a gap is present to link these individuals to the companies wishing to hire or develop a skilled workforce with innovative postsecondary delivery options.

Despite the compelling charge for change from community stakeholders, employers, and workers; the leveraging of significant resources from state and local partners; the development of a noteworthy integrated workforce system; and attainment of promising early outcomes, OCTC remains an institution in transition. The traditions of academia are rigid and age old. Major gaps and shortcomings must be overlaid to sustain the integrated, flexible delivery model critical to the low-skilled working adult's success in navigating the academic gauntlet. Moving an academic delivery model perceived as having too much unrelated, unvalued work to a more relevant contextually based, modular and credentialed learning requires four key strategies: (1) Offering academic programs and support services with sufficient flexibility for working adults, (2) retaining at-risk students and fostering their success, (3) effectively reaching underserved populations (low-skilled, low-income, minorities) for inclusion in the program, and (4) sustaining the program by successfully facilitating a culture change throughout the college.

The Kentucky Workforce Investment Board's state planning group identified three career clusters that will create future high demand for skilled workers in the Commonwealth: manufacturing, health care, and hospitality. Collaborative discussions between agency partners, training providers, and industry stakeholders have elicited great interest and enthusiasm to address all three career cluster opportunities within the community. However, one statistic was particularly compelling to planning partners: that a significant portion of the region's labor market (19.5% total; 15.6% in Daviess County alone) was engaged in the manufacturing sector. These data, along with a strategic analysis of recent expansions and job growth, company training activity, wage potential (Daviess County local average of $690 per week), and economic impact, led to a strong group consensus to address manufacturing as Greater Owensboro's first career pathway.

THE PARTNERS

Four partners worked together in various capacities in the past, but they developed a streamlined system of communication and collaboration to implement the new pathways program. The existing barriers that prevented collaboration before were an unstated competitiveness for funding; the approval of academic programming that meets company needs, not just those of the academic institution; and the lack of a modularized, portable system to build credentialing for postsecondary attainment through technical training. The four partners, whose involvement was essential in the development and implementation of the Advanced Manufacturing for the 21st Century pathway model, were as follows:

OCTC (training provider). The college's CCED provided a highly integrated workforce development delivery system with a wide array of programs and services. In addition to continuing education, customized training, and assessment services, CCED's Center for Technical Excellence offered industry partners a unique range of mobile training capabilities, experienced trainers, and other resources critical for incumbent worker skill enhancement. CCED was able to support basic skills, ESL, WorkKeys, and other skill and training needs of unemployed and underemployed individuals through its SkillTrain Adult Learning Center. The college's SkillTrain initiative, with its dual customers of workers and employers, emphasized the need to link low-skilled adults to technical training with the labor market payoffs. Participants gained adult basic education skills through the contextually based WorkKeys system, but had little ability to access traditionally delivered technical course work. CCED's integrated approach for its programs and services coupled with the college's excellent industrial maintenance faculty and curriculum ensured that the Advanced Manufacturing for the 21st Century pathway model had the foundation for success.

OCTC was chosen to participate in a system-led, Ford Foundation career pathway project. Known as IMAC (Industry Modular Accessible Credentials), the initiative launched with a credit-bearing, modularized electrical certificate imbedded in the associate degree for industrial maintenance. A blended delivery approach (Web-based and instructor led) with extensive open lab hours allows participants self-paced, competency-based learning. The opportunity to learn at a faster pace, to complete Web-based course work anytime and anywhere, and to demonstrate and receive credit for knowledge already attained has generated tremendous excitement among the first generation of participants.

The Department for Employment Services, the Green River Area Development District, the Owensboro One-Stop and Other Agency Members (community agencies). As was stated earlier, these local community services agencies provided employability skills training, job search assistance, referral services, counseling, transportation, child care, and other important assistance related to elimination of barriers to participation.

The Greater Owensboro Economic Development Corporation and the Greater Owensboro Chamber of Commerce. The primary focus of these organizations is the promotion of economic growth through the development of strategies and resources required to support current and future workforce needs of the Greater Owensboro area. Both organizations participated in and supported the development of the manufacturing/industrial maintenance pathway model.

DANA Corporation, Weyerhaeuser, Aleris, Century Aluminum, Kimberly Clark, Unilever (business and industry). The primary focus of industry partners is to utilize the career pathways model for hiring and incumbent worker skill enhancement, to develop and participate in collaboratively developed technical training programs, to recognize project credentials in employment and promotion practices, and to actively assist in the modularization of the curriculum.

IMPLEMENTATION

The OCTC Career Pathway Implementation Team (comprised of faculty and CCED staff) spent a considerable amount of time seeking business and industry input, researching and visiting other colleges for best practices, investigating delivery methods, and testing vendors of multimedia learning products. OCTC teamed up with Amatrol, Inc. (headquartered in Jeffersonville, Indiana), a leading vendor of multimedia training programs and equipment to offer a flexible, self-paced model for learning. Amatrol's Web-based learning modules and hands-on lab program matched closely with the task lists and competencies of the college's existing manufacturing curriculum.

At the beginning of August 2005, OCTC launched a pilot program for dislocated workers to earn an "accelerated" credential while preparing for a new job search. A consortium group of incumbent workers was launched in early fall 2006. Currently, 26 students are enrolled in the IMAC industrial maintenance career pathways pilot credit courses delivered through a blended approach of Web-based learning combined with face-to-face instructional support and hands-on lab activities. Three credentials were established:

- Industrial Maintenance Electrical Mechanic Certificate: 22 Credits
- Industrial Maintenance Technician Diploma: 48–60 credits
- Associate in applied science degree: 60–76 credits

To begin the program, students need WorkKeys scores in applied mathematics, reading for information, and locating information at the Silver KEC level (level 4 in each of the three areas). WorkKeys and KECs are available at no charge through OCTC's SkillTrain. Next, students are required to attend a brief orientation session that provides a complete overview of the program.

In January 2006, an open lab concept for industrial maintenance was launched. Students in OCTC's traditional academic program, career pathways program, and business and industry training program now share this lab, which houses equipment for electrical, mechanical, and electronics exercises. The lab is managed by three faculty members, an instructional lab facilitator, and an industry trainer. At least one of the five is present when students are in the lab to ensure quality of instruction and safety of equipment use. This open lab concept allows students to complete required exercises at their own pace, make up any work missed, and obtain additional instructional assistance if needed.

LESSONS LEARNED

Through formal and informal evaluations, the students in the pilot group reported that they enjoy taking the career pathway classes because of the scheduling flexibility, self-paced option, small-group learning activities, and the helpfulness of the instructor and instructional assistant. They like the Web-based modules because they combine the same academic theory and concepts covered in OCTC's traditional courses with state-of-the-art graphics and interactive simulations and videos. The students also reported that the additional instructor-led workshops and hands on lab exercises have helped them learn and practice skills that will be valuable to them in the workplace. The components of the development and implementation of the Advanced Manufacturing for the 21st Century career pathways model are summarized in Table 15.1.

The key issues that were identified for the program's success are as follows:

- **Open entry.** Students should be able to register for courses at any time of the year, even after the official deadline for traditional registration has ended.
- **Open exit.** Students should be able to complete a course at any time of the year and have their grade entered into PeopleSoft.
- **Financial aid.** The ability to record an *MP* (making progress) grade instead of an *I* for students working on a module or course after the traditional semester ends is needed to fulfill financial aid guidelines requiring a report of satisfactory progress.
- **Tuition.** A specialized rate structure is needed that addresses the additional cost of delivering highly flexible module courses, including the expense incurred with managing the program; offering Web-based learning to serve multiple students simultaneously; the expanded hours of labs; and the additional availability of instructional assistance.
- **Tuition refund policy.** Flexibility in the tuition refund policy is needed so that transactions are not tied to a traditional academic semester.

Table 15.1	Components of the Manufacturing Career Pathways Model at OCTC
Delivery System	CD-Rom based or Web-based (to allow for networking) Availability of updates to purchased curriculum Need of personal instruction and coaching
Tracking/Assessment	Evaluation of student progress Reporting capabilities for administrator
Learning Center Design	Up-to-date computer stations (system requirements) Server for curriculum and tracking management program Other equipment needs such as printers, copiers, etc.
Hands-on Training Lab	Equipment needed to facilitate skill demonstration Qualified lab assistant with knowledge of programs
Student Success	Orientation for groups and individuals Learning contract with start dates, expected completion dates, and time management plans Coaching and mentoring opportunities Encouragement notices to keep students on task (phone calls, post cards, etc.)
Personnel	Coordination, faculty availability, coaching, assistants Faculty loads
Student Services	Enrollment policies and procedures Financial aid opportunities Grading practices Transcript issues Advising

Brownfields Training Program Readies Environmental Workers in North Carolina

Fran Daniel

Community colleges play an important role in helping people qualify for careers in a so-called green industry, that is, to help environmental workers. This case study describes such a socially relevant program.

As an environmental technician at 3RC, a waste-management company in Winston-Salem, Keisha Roper's job consists of unloading household hazardous waste, recycling waste, and doing just whatever needs to be done. It is not always the most glamorous type of work, but it is a job that Roper, who has a bachelor's degree in art from Winston-Salem State University, said she wanted to do after she completed a program that trains workers for jobs in environmentally related fields. When Roper entered the Winston-Salem Brownfields Environmental Job Training Program in early 2003, life had not been too kind. A recent college graduate, she had gone for months working temporary jobs for a few hours of pay at a time. "I was feeling hopeless," she said. But things turned around when 3RC hired her just a few days after she completed the Brownfields training program. "I feel like the program gave a lot of people an opportunity to be employed, because everybody pretty much that was in my class had been unemployed for quite some time," she said. "Quite a few people out of my class got jobs at the end, and that was really positive, because it's like you go from no job to a job. It was very beneficial."

Begun in 2000 under a grant from the U.S. Environmental Protection Agency, the Winston-Salem Brownfields Environmental Job Training Program provides environmental training, skills, and certification. The city has two partners to help administer the program: Forsyth Technical Community College, Winston-Salem, North Carolina, and The Northwest Piedmont Council of Governments' Workforce Development program. The first Brownfields program training class was held in 2002. Since then, it has had 43 graduates, including one tuition student. "Brownfields refers to a concept of properties being reused rather than creating, for example, new industrial or commercial sites from greenfields," said Tim Binkley the Brownfields job training coordinator. The program's focus is on the residents of the Liberty Street corridor, from approximately the north edge of downtown to Smith Reynolds Airport, and other unemployed or underemployed adults who want new skills and a career in environmentally related businesses.

Tim Binkley said that the goal of the program is to provide specialized skills to people wanting a new career path in environmentally related industries and to provide a workforce with skills to meet the evolving needs in environmental management. He said that its long-term goal is to become self-sustaining so that an employer such as the city, a consulting firm, or a hospital can send employees who are short on skills to the program to bring them up to speed and to provide jobs for the community. During the past 3 years, various departments of the city of Winston-Salem, Forsyth County Environmental Affairs, 3RC, Engineering Tectonics PA of Winston-Salem, and Geoscience & Technology PA of Winston-Salem have been just a few of the participants in the program who have been involved in such activities as apprenticeships, job fairs, or training. The current curriculum of 210 hours of classroom and field teaching provides students with a wide spectrum of issues concerning environmental practice and management in three areas—air, water, and soil. Binkley said that the health and safety section, which includes 40 hours of hazardous waste training, is what employers are most interested in.

Michele Sakwa, the president of 3RC, which has been in the program since it started and has hired approximately five of its graduates, said that it is a big deal to hire a person with 40 hours of hazardous training and certification. "That's a premium person." She said that she was happy to get Roper as an employee because Roper is such a fast learner. Mike Taber, who is now an environmental technician for ECS Ltd. in Greensboro, was one of the first graduates of the Brownfields program. Like Roper, he had never worked in the environmental industry. "The program is going to give you the basic skills you need," said Taber, who previously worked approximately 25 years in the construction industry. "If you take them and apply them with good work ethics, I think any company would like to have the trainees from the program." Brian Maas, the environmental-business manager for ECS, said he is pleased with Taber's work and would hire another student from the program if the company should hire another candidate in the future. "The program itself I feel is a great program," he said. "The participants who successfully complete the program come in better trained than somebody that you would possibly have to hire and guess whether or not they would work out for you."

The year that Taber worked for ECS, there was additional money through the Workforce Development program from the U.S. Department of Labor to pay for several months of job training at a company, including ECS. Craig Spry, a utility plant operator for the city–county's Thomas Water Treatment Plant, graduated from the program this year. As an entry-level operator, Spry described his job as more of a mental challenge than a physical challenge because there is so much to learn and keep up with. "We check things constantly throughout the whole day," he said. "That's to make sure that our quality control standards are being followed. That way we can make sure that we are sending out the best drinking water to the public." Edward Davis, the plant supervisor, said he was glad to get Spry as an employee. "When I looked at his application, I noticed that he had this environment training," he said. "At the time, I was looking for an individual that I felt could apply himself to this type of job and that seemed to fit right into my program. I've been pretty pleased."

Note. From "Winston-Salem, N.C., Brownfields Training Program Readies Environmental Workers," by F. Daniel, August 10, 2004, *Knight Ridder Tribune Business News*, p. 1. Copyright 2004 by TMS Reprints. Adapted with permission.

CASE 17

Encouraging Careers in Manufacturing

Anne C. Lewis

Community colleges play a role in interesting young people in occupational entry. This case study describes such a program focused on manufacturing.

The National Association of Manufacturers (NAM) has launched a 10-year effort to encourage young people to prepare for and work in manufacturing. A study commissioned by NAM found an alarming disinterest in manufacturing careers among young people, even though the Baby Boom retirement will create a need for 10 million additional skilled manufacturing workers by 2020. A previous NAM survey concluded that a crisis in the supply of qualified workers already exists. More than 80% of the manufacturers surveyed reported a current shortage of qualified job applicants. The more recent study, *Keeping America Competitive: How a Talent Shortage Threatens U.S. Manufacturing* (2003), attributed the looming problem to two factors: (1) the negative and inaccurate perceptions of young people, their parents, and school counselors about careers in manufacturing, and (2) the lack of educational preparation that would help young people acquire the skills they need for manufacturing jobs.

Young people tend to view manufacturing jobs as "dark, dreary, and dead end," according to Phyllis Eisen, executive director of the Center for Workforce Success at NAM. They see them as rote work on an assembly line. Moreover, they believe manufacturing is in decline because jobs are moving overseas. Finally, their perceptions of manufacturing careers do not fit with the kind of work they want—creative, emotionally and financially rewarding, and with opportunities to climb a career ladder. Students do not receive proper career guidance about manufacturing employment, the study pointed out. Guidance counselors do not have enough information about job opportunities and spend most of their time helping students apply for college. The study blames both the manufacturing sector and the education system for not providing useful information about the manufacturing workplace.

To have a large enough applicant pool for its requirements, Intel now focuses on the pipeline at community colleges, according to Rito Martinez, the Intel workforce development and college recruiting manager in Colorado. Speaking at a forum in Washington, D.C., where the NAM report was discussed, he said the 2-year degree programs were good sources of employees, especially minorities and women, who could be put on a career path in manufacturing. However, budget cutbacks and negative perceptions of manufacturing jobs hinder efforts to recruit a sufficient number of young people through community college programs. Martinez said basic skills still are necessary, but his industry also needs people who are well grounded in math, science, and technology; teamwork skills; and industriousness.

A community college official from Colorado confirmed both the sets of skills needed in manufacturing and the misconceptions that young people, their parents, and school counselors have of manufacturing jobs. Tom Heywood, education outreach coordinator at Pikes Peak Community College, also said that teachers and counselors direct students away from manufacturing careers and toward 4-year college programs. Heywood was able to change perceptions of some teachers and counselors by hosting workshops in which they visited manufacturing workplaces.

The NAM long-range effort, according to Eisen, is known as the Campaign for Growth and Manufacturing Renewal. It will promote manufacturing careers as a preferred option through public awareness, career planning resources, and a public education campaign.

References

Keeping America Competitive: How a Talent Shortage Threatens U.S. Manufacturing. (2003). Retrieved January, 2007, from www.nam.org/s_nam/sec.asp?CID=84&DID=82

Note. From "Encouraging Careers in Manufacturing," by C. Lewis, 2003, *Tech Directions, 63*(1), p. 5. Copyright 2005 by Prakken Publications, Inc. Adapted with permission.

CASE *18*

Economic Development Office Provides Career Development to Entrepreneurs in Virginia

Meghann Cotter

Community colleges play a role in offering career development to entrepreneurs, a key group in small business formation. This case study describes such a program, which is of growing interest in the United States.

Business owners wanting to set up shop in Stafford County, Virginia, now have access to extra help. The county's Office of Economic Development is offering an interactive compact disk (CD) as a tutor for those wanting to relocate or start a business in the area. This kind of CD is offered by only six other Virginia localities. The CD includes information about the community, such as infrastructure, labor, minority enterprise, and tax details. It also provides a step-by-step process for starting and operating a business. It has software that allows people to plug in information to create a printable business plan.

The county used to distribute a brochure that listed basic demographic data as well as offices that could help people start or expand their businesses. But that method required users to go to several different places to collect the information. Stafford's new product is designed to put all the necessary information at a business owner's fingertips. The CD format for the data, first released in February 2004 by the Community College Workforce Alliance and Center for Entrepreneurial Development in Richmond, is gaining popularity. The organization is currently working on CDs for two other counties. Further, they have about a dozen other requests, including locations in North Carolina. The counties already participating have a difficult time keeping the CDs in stock. Henrico County, for example, ordered 1,300 copies, thinking that would last the county a year. But staff members had to reorder more just 4 months later.

Statistics from the Coffman Foundation, which was established to encourage entrepreneurial activity throughout the United States, show that 43% of people have seriously thought about starting their own business. Most, however, give up because they find the process to be too complicated, said Stu Neal, a founder of the CD technology at the Community College Workforce Alliance. That information served as the inspiration behind his idea. "We wanted to make it easy for people [who want to start businesses] to go out and get questions answered," Neal said. He said his product is written at the high school or graduate equivalency diploma level so that anyone can read and understand what they need to do. To further the education of business owners, Neal and his staff are working to perfect an 8-week training program that goes along with the CD. When completed, they plan to offer it at community colleges throughout the state.

Tim Baroody, Stafford County's director of economic development, hopes the CD will lure business to the area. But his primary goal is to equip potential and existing small businesses with the tools to succeed. His office gets several inquiries from aspiring business owners each week, he said. It is not always possible to sit down and assist each one. The CD will enable Baroody's office to give businesses the more immediate help they need. It contains contact information and links to other organizations if people need technical assistance or have other questions. "It's a way to take them by the hand and show them exactly what they need to do to set up," said Cathy Riddle, Stafford County's public information officer.

Small businesses—those with fewer than 50 employees—already make up approximately 90% of business in Stafford. "Small businesses provide anything from coffee to lumber, and anything in between. And we are grateful that they provide added resources and employment for our community," Baroody said. He said he wants to raise awareness of where Stafford is and what it has to offer. "It's not that we are far off in the boonies. We are just down the street," Baroody said. "And we're open for business."

Note. From "Stafford County, Va., Economic Development Office Provides CD to Entrepreneurs," by M. Cotter, December 16, 2004, *Knight Ridder Tribune Business News*, p. 1. Copyright 2004 by TMS Reprints. Adapted with permission.

PART 4

Case Studies of Community Colleges Supporting Community Development

Community colleges play an important role in building social capital by providing a focal point for community development. The cases in this section emphasize that role.

Case 19. Effective Community Involvement and Partnerships

Case 20. Building Business Partnerships

Case 21. Housatonic Community College Brings Employees and Businesses Together

Case 22. Local Demand Should Drive Community College Efforts

CASE *19*

Effective Community Involvement and Partnerships

Trenton Wright

Community colleges play a role in community development. This case study describes how community colleges are well equipped to provide the specialized skills and certifications required by the U.S. Environmental Protection Agency for Brownfield site cleanup.

ailed as legislation to clean up the environment and create jobs, the Small Business Liability Relief and Brownfields Revitalization Act of 2002 helps states and communities around the country clean up and revitalize Brownfields sites. The president's FY 2003 budget contained $200 million for Brownfields Economic Redevelopment.

BROWNFIELDS BACKGROUND

The U.S. Environmental Protection Agency (EPA) defines a Brownfield site as one that is underused because of a real or perceived presence of hazardous materials. Brownfields are abandoned, idle, or underused industrial and commercial facilities where expansion or redevelopment is complicated by real or perceived environmental contamination. Since its inception in 1995, the Brownfields program has awarded 645 grants to assess Brownfields sites and to make loans to conduct cleanups. Every acre of reclaimed Brownfields saves 4.5 acres of green space such as park and recreation areas, according to EPA estimates. More than 430 Brownfields Assessment Pilots (communities that have received the equivalent of planning grants) are recognized by EPA. New assessment and cleanup sites are added to the EPA list for funding at the rate of 50 to 60 per year.

All workers who enter these sites for assessment or cleanup activities must possess certain specialized unique skills and certifications. Agencies affiliated with these pilot sites also have the opportunity to compete for EPA Brownfields Worker Training Grants. These grants typically last 2 years and provide up to $200,000 for workforce training and related activities. EPA awards new grants yearly through a highly competitive grant application process.

TRAINING OPPORTUNITIES

In January 2002, President Bush signed into law the Small Business Liability Relief and Brownfields Revitalization Act, which authorized up to $250 million per year for Brownfields grants, including up to $50 million for the assessment and cleanup of low-risk, petroleum-contaminated sites. The new legislation allows EPA to provide training to expedite assessment, remediation, and preparation of Brownfields sites.

The job training grants are used to teach environmental cleanup job skills to people living in low-income areas near Brownfields sites. Applicants for the job training program must be located in or near a community that currently receives, or has received, financial assistance from EPA for Brownfields-related activities. A majority of participants who successfully complete the training program go on to pursue careers with environmental firms and organizations.

Local Workforce Investment Boards and One-Stop Career Centers

Local workforce investment boards (LWIB) located near Brownfields sites are encouraged to apply for Brownfields Worker Training Grants. Currently, approximately 30 sites are receiving these funds from EPA. Of the 10 new grants awarded in May 2003, 5 were submitted by LWIBs or One-Stop Career Centers. Three others cited the LWIB as a partner. The Workplace, Inc., representing southwest Connecticut, is a recent EPA awardee and will serve 11 communities with identified Brownfields located in the lower Naugatuck River Valley. Groundwork Providence, also a recent awardee, just received $25,000 from its Providence Workforce Board to supplement its program.

Communities and economic development officials prefer local residents to work on publicly funded remediation projects. Training and employment needs at Brownfields sites hold tremendous opportunities for LWIBs, local training providers, and the citizens served by the U.S. Department of Labor through the Workforce Investment Act. Through coordination with the local agency in charge of these Brownfields sites, LWIBs and One-Stop Career Centers can help to ensure that local workers are qualified for these jobs when the project begins. Through this type of collaboration, performance measures of the local board and those of the local grantee can be mutually enhanced because both groups are working toward the shared goal of training and employing local workers.

Another benefit of this type of collaboration is that the LWIB or One-Stop Career Center is involved with planning officials at the earliest stages of site planning. This allows workforce professionals at the local level to participate in planning for the job readiness needs for the site's use after its cleanup. As a result, workforce agencies enhance their ability to provide needed services to the businesses, industries, or agencies that will be the next tenants of these properties.

ENVIRONMENTAL JUSTICE

The EPA Brownfields Job Training Program requires a strong environmental justice component. Many of the contaminated sites nationally are located in minority and low-income neighborhoods. In October 1999, the Council for Urban Economic Development released a study confirming that EPA's Brownfields Initiative is being put to use in the communities that need it most: blighted communities of racial and ethnic minorities and low-income citizens. A common thread across these programs is the effective use of advisory committees to broaden community representation and participation in program design and implementation.

MID-CONNECTICUT BROWNFIELDS JOB TRAINING PILOT

To promote economic revitalization and safeguard the environment and public health, the EPA awarded Middlesex Community College (MxCC), Middletown, Connecticut, one of the first Brownfields Job Training Grants under the Small Business Liability Relief and Brownfields Revitalization Act of 2002. Middletown was also 1 of 10 communities in seven states that each received $200,000 EPA grants to provide environmental job training at Brownfields sites. This was MxCC's second EPA Brownfields Job Training Grant.

The MxCC project, called the Mid-Connecticut Brownfields Job Training Pilot, plans to train 100 students over 2 years, achieve an 82% job placement rate, and track graduates for 18 months after job placement. The target participants will be underemployed or unemployed residents of nine central Connecticut communities: Middletown, Meriden, Portland, Cromwell, New Britain, Southington, Cheshire, Haddam, and Wallingford. Placement in environmental jobs will be accomplished through the community college's existing relationships with the many technical employers in the area. The MxCC training program uses a customized training component with a flexibly scheduled 40-hour, and three college credit, Occupational Safety and Health Administration course.

The project focuses on partnerships with nine communities, environmental industry employers, and community-based organizations. The project area has a population of 312,252 and covers 265 square miles. The project receives direction through an advisory committee that encompasses the following diverse entities within the nine contiguous communities: Middlesex National Association for the

Advancement of Colored People (NAACP), Meriden NAACP, New Britain NAACP, Middlesex County Soil and Water Conservation District, Enviromed, Marin Environmental, Vanasse Hangen Brustlin, Inc., North End Action Team (the Middletown-based community action agency), New Opportunities of Greater Meriden (the Meriden community action agency), Northeast Utilities System, New England Training and Consulting, Tighe & Bond Inc., Clearwater Systems EEC, and the Connecticut Department of Labor.

Although MxCC used a smaller advisory committee for its previous 2-year Brownfields award, a larger committee was needed to serve an expanded geographic area, reach deeper into neighborhoods, and involve more community-based organizations and the NAACP chapters in the current training program. This expanded outreach also included bilingual recruiting material to gain better representation from the significant Latino populations in New Britain and Meriden, which is estimated at 31,100 people. Northeast Utilities, a major public utility, was included because of its increasing focus on promoting economic development and sensitivity for environmental concerns in its service area.

This initiative joins three area NAACP chapters to assist in recruiting minority populations that may not be reached by traditional marketing methods. With median incomes within Brownfields Pilot–targeted areas at 30% below the national average, the initiative mirrors EPA's focus on the impact of environmental pollution on disadvantaged segments of society. Roxanne Aaron-Selph, president of the Middletown NAACP chapter, stated, "Over the past decade, the NAACP has invested considerable resources in the area of advocacy for safe environment for families. The NAACP has always viewed the academic and business communities as integral parts of the economic solution to the problems which frustrate the African American community. Middlesex Community College has designed a comprehensive educational training program to reach the underserved." Aaron-Selph now serves as the chairperson of the current MxCC Project Advisory Committee.

For the 2003 submission, MxCC concluded that a low-tech (shorter length and less academic focus) approach would be the most successful. Program administration was transferred out of academics to the business and industry department, the training modules length was cut in half, the number of trainees was doubled, another off-site location was added, and the service area was more than doubled. The current EPA project will leverage approximately $91,000 of in-kind support over 2 years from the college and other citizen group supporters. The previous 2-year award, in 2000 to 2002, leveraged $100,000 in in-kind resources.

The additional training site in Meriden was added to expand the participation of citizens in the larger communities of Meriden (58,000), New Britain (71,000), and Wallingford (42,000). Reducing the transportation distance and costs for low- and moderate-income participants in these geographic areas was a key factor in selecting a second training site.

The grant is administered through the college's Center for Business and Industry Services, one of the original centers in the statewide Business & Industry Services Network. The Center for Business and Industry Service provides companies throughout Middlesex County and the Meriden-Wallingford area with a full range of customized training, instruction, and consultation services. MxCC serves approximately 2,400 full- and part-time students.

OTHER COMMUNITY-BASED PARTNERSHIPS AND BEST PRACTICES

Other Brownfields training programs have employed community partnerships to enhance their effectiveness. Most of these programs have used a broadly representative advisory committee to expand community participation and build stronger partnerships.

New Jersey Youth Corps

EPA initially selected the New Jersey Youth Corps for a Brownfields Job Training and Development Demonstration Pilot in 1998. Both Camden and Newark are Brownfields Assessment Demonstration Pilots and state urban enterprise zones, and the populations of both are primarily minorities. Camden is also a federal empowerment zone. The New Jersey Youth Corps provides a program that enabled 60 out-of-school youth to obtain a high school equivalency diploma and gain job readiness skills through community service. The program provides strong community partnerships at the local program site, so the connection to employment and job-related opportunities is strong. In addition, the New Jersey Youth Corps has a partnership with the New Jersey Institute of Technology, broadening access to environmental agencies interested in interns or employees from the program. Another critical component was the collaboration and support provided by the EPA Region II Brownfields project manager. Strong linkages with the community at large, educational institutions, and EPA personnel and a good reputation within the local communities were all key components to the success of this pilot project. They were selected again in 2000 to serve the Middlesex County, New Jersey, area. The New Jersey Youth Corps also received another pilot 2-year grant in 2003 for the Phillipsburg–Newark area and has added a biotechnology component to the curriculum.

Coalition for a Better Acre: Lowell, MA

Coalition for a Better Acre, a community development corporation (CDC) formed in 1982, received an EPA award in 2003 and is using an advisory committee to represent various interests within the city's population of approximately 110,000. The advisory board consists of three environmental technology companies, two professors, one municipal official, one member of the Cambodian community, one faith-based representative, and one resident. The project will leverage $82,400 in non-EPA funds.

Jobs for Youth Networks: Boston, MA

JFY Networks is a nonprofit workforce development agency serving greater Boston since 1976. In 2003, it received its third, 2-year EPA award. The agency is using a 15-member advisory board with representatives from environmental technology companies, a labor union, a community-based organization, a social security agency, and other state and federal representatives. The advisory board consists of Clean Harbors (a large national remediation company) and the president of the Environmental Business Council of New England. The agency also maintains a strong relationship with Boston municipal officials regarding the program. They have a good record of providing environmental training programs since 1995.

Groundwork Providence Brownfields Job Training and Development Program

EPA selected Groundwork Providence, a private nonprofit organization, as a grant recipient in December 2001. This is the first, and to date the only, program of its kind in Rhode Island. Providence is a city of 25 neighborhoods; a majority of its 173,600 residents are minorities. The job training pilot focuses on three federal enterprise community neighborhoods that are predominantly minority populations and that have poverty rates as high as 47%. Groundwork Providence is a community-based organization whose mission is to bring about sustained regeneration, improvement, and management of the physical environment by developing community-based partnerships that empower people, businesses, and organizations to promote environmental, economic, and social well-being.

The principal program partners include the Rhode Island Economic Development Corporation, the Rhode Island Department of Environmental Management, the Providence Department of Planning and Development, the Community College of Rhode Island, and Workforce Solutions of Providence/Cranston (the LWIB). The project uses an 18-member advisory board to ensure community participation; the advisory board includes a representative from each agency previously mentioned, plus Genesis Center (a literacy and immigrant support agency), Federal Hill House (a childcare agency), the International Institute (a language skills and citizenship support agency), Dorcas Place (a women and children support agency), Travelers Aid Society (a homeless and community outreach agency), Stop Wasting Abandoned Property (a CDC), and several employer representatives. To date, 72 trainees have completed training. Groundwork Providence also was awarded $150,000 to conduct its program in the Pawtucket, Rhode Island, area.

City of Stamford, Connecticut

This pilot program trained 35 participants recruited from Stamford's primarily minority and distressed Waterside and South End neighborhoods (population 8,300), which are located in a state enterprise zone on the shores of Long Island Sound. In the pilot area, the South End population is 44% African American and

35% Hispanic, with an average per capita income that is less than half of the city-wide average. The Waterside population is 77% minority and has a 25% poverty rate and a higher-than-average unemployment rate. There are numerous Brown-fields interspersed with commercial and residential properties. The city is con-ducting a comprehensive revitalization effort in these communities, including a Dock Street Connector project that will improve transportation to the harbor area. The economic distress of South End and Waterside and the revitalization efforts of the city indicated a need for environmental training in these two neighbor-hoods.

The city's training effort was supported by organizations such as CTE, Inc. (a community action agency for the city), Norwalk Community Technical College, EnviroMed Services, Inc., the Stamford Area Commerce and Industry Associa-tion, and the Waterside Coalition. The state enterprise zone designation requires environmental contractors to hire local residents. Half the students in the training program came from the South End and Waterside, the two areas targeted because of their long history as industrial sites. The success of the program was dependent on the partnerships.

BEST PRACTICES

Successful job development requires the involvement of all parties that could in-fluence the program at the partner level. Commitment and teamwork from the partners, as well as good intercommunication among the partners, is imperative. The trick to establishing partnerships is transforming people with different goals into a cohesive group that will strongly advocate for the job development program. Given the varied interests of different partners, it is important to build consensus among the group. The work of MxCC revealed numerous best practices to estab-lish community partnerships and implement a successful Brownfields job training program. These effective practices include the following:

- Coordinate with the local business association.
- Involve local churches.
- Involve community development corporations, Job Training Partnership Act, and empowerment or enterprise zones.
- Involve state and federal health and human services agencies.
- Involve community-based organizations.
- Involve local boards of education.
- Conduct outreach to the community to inform the public about the Brown-fields initiatives.
- Involve the mayor's office, other elected officials, and chambers of commerce.
- Focus on program sustainability after the grant.
- Develop potential funding strategies.

- Create high visibility in the mayor's office.
- Create high visibility within congressional district.
- Involve private-sector partners.
- Change the mindset of the organization, which requires time away from the office to network
- Tie the project to local and regional economic development plans.
- Develop or partner with the Brownfields working group to conduct outreach to communities within the project service area.
- Involve the National Environmental Justice Advisory Council.
- Educate citizens about the Brownfields process and job opportunities through a "Brownfields Basics" course.
- Involve all Brownfields stakeholders, civic organizations, and the city planning and development office.
- Offer employers tax credits.
- Use the EPA's Web site for information on environmental justice groups.
- Partner with the Army Corps of Engineers.

CONCLUSION

Community colleges have long understood the importance of collaborating, but the prolonged downturn in the economy has made them even more eager to partner with others. If necessity is the mother of invention, a poor economy is the mother of collaboration. Scarcity of resources and a need to be responsive to local community concerns forces community colleges to partner with others. Two recent national studies, the U.S. General Accounting Offices report on workforce development and the Ford Foundations report, Driving Change in Community Colleges (prepared by Jobs for the Future), both concluded that the most successful colleges, especially in workforce development, are those that have learned to collaborate with multiple partners for a common goal.

Community colleges bring experience in education, training, faculties, curriculum, support services, and substantial in-kind support to Brownfields projects. Community colleges have considerable experience working with nontraditional students and cater to vocational career tracks. Reaching these local citizens may be easier with noncredit or customized job training areas of the community college rather than relying solely on an academic orientation.

Pilot communities should form an advisory board or committee that consists of a diverse group of local stakeholders to guide the project and enhance community networking activities. Pilot communities also should work to include the local community college and the LWIB in program planning and implementation, because these entities help leverage limited federal funds. The same collaborative and partnership strategies that ensure citizen group participation in Brownfields programs also can be used in other workforce development initiatives.

Across all pilot communities researched by the International City Managers Association, the Brownfields Job Training Programs were managed by one lead organization, but incorporated partnerships with local stakeholders that included local governments, nonprofit associations, CDCs, private firms, and academic institutions. The expertise, support, and resources of the job training programs were key to the success of most programs. Local governments, especially small and mid-sized communities, may not be the most appropriate entity to manage a Brownfields Job Training Program. Experience in workforce development may be the most appropriate criteria to lead such an effort.

Partnerships and collaboration clearly demonstrate the ability to leverage resources and enhance restricted and limited federal funding. Since the Brownfields Worker Training Program started in 1998, EPA has awarded 56 pilot grants totaling $10.7 million. Through these grants, 1,366 people have completed training, and 903 program participants have obtained jobs in the environmental field that pay an average hourly wage of $12.55. According to an independent study conducted by the Council for Economic Development, the revitalization of Brownfields has created 22,000 permanent jobs and leveraged $2.48 in private investment for every dollar spent by federal, state, or local governments.

Note. From "Effective Community Involvement and Partnerships," by T. Wright, 2004, *Economic Development Journal, 3*(3), pp. 26–32. Copyright 2005 by International Economic Development Council. Adapted with permission.

CASE *20*

Building Business Partnerships

BusinessWest

This case study illustrates how one community college takes a proactive approach to identifying the future needs of industry to better meet worker training needs and secure funding.

According to Geoff Little, area employers have been asked many times—and in many ways—to project into the future, assess where their specific sectors are going, and gauge what skills their employees will need. "People tell us that they keep being asked, 'What do you need? What do you need? What do you need?'" said Little, adding that what has been missing from the equation in many ways has been adequate response to the answers from those queries.

THE PROJECT: PREDICT THE FUTURE

Providing timely, appropriate response is one of the many goals behind an ambitious undertaking on the part of Springfield Technical Community College (STCC) in Springfield, Massachusetts. According to Little, the project's leader, who has recently served as a consultant on a number of regional economic development initiatives, the Business Partnership Development Program, as it is called, is designed to garner specific information about where several area business clusters are headed in terms of everything from foreign competition to needed employee skill sets.

He told *BusinessWest* the business partnership project has involved hiring the

Utah-based Clements Group, which specializes in mentoring clients, including 500 community colleges nationwide, to envision, analyze, and quantify needs; analyze funding sources; and then develop strategies for meeting stated goals. The initiative is being undertaken in response to outlined priorities contained within the region's Plan for Progress, which was updated last year, and it was inspired by President Bush's call last year for the nation's community colleges to take on a larger role in workforce development initiatives.

"Federal money will soon become available for specific projects that fall in this realm," said Gail Carberry, the school's vice president of grants and development. With information gleaned from the business partnership, the college should be better positioned to win some of that funding, she added. Information is now starting to come in.

Representatives of several clusters have come together for forums at the college over the past few months. These groups include hospitals (14 representatives of area facilities, including Hank Porten, president and chief executive officer of Holyoke Medical Center, and Charles Cavagnaro, president and chief executive officer of Wing Memorial Hospital were in attendance) and two sessions of manufacturers—those with fewer than 100 employees and those with more than that number.

"Data and comments are being organized into comprehensive reports," said Little, noting that this is only the first step in the process. What follows is work to prioritize identified needs and develop strategies to meet them. Steps could run the gamut from minor curriculum adjustments to an expansion of existing academic offerings to creation of new programs. "What happens, and how soon, will be a function of priority and resources," said Carberry, noting that STCC president, Ira Rubenzahl, who took office last summer, made it one of his priorities to collaborate with area businesses to ensure that the workforce of the future was adequately equipped with the skills it would need.

WORK IN PROGRESS

Little, a member of the executive committee of the STCC foundation board, which agreed to split the $18,000 cost of the project, said the word to focus on is "partnership." He told *Business West* that the process of assessing needs and crafting responses will be ongoing, with information-gathering sessions occurring perhaps on an annual basis with some clusters. The goal is to generate a running communitywide dialogue that will help the school—and perhaps other area colleges as well—more effectively anticipate and then meet the broad and specific needs of area companies and industry groups. STCC is focusing on those sectors in which it specializes: primarily health care, manufacturing, and engineering technology, among others. The school has advisory boards that work to identify industry needs and curriculum priorities, Little explained, but these groups operate in what he called "real time."

Methodology

What the college needed was a format that would project needs further into the future; for that, it turned to the Clements Group. The 20-year-old company works primarily with community colleges and technical institutes, although it also provides assistance in resource development for K–12 systems and related foundations. For colleges, the Clements Group offers an array of services, including strategic planning, institutional development assessment, fundraising campaigns, image and marketing services, feasibility studies, and foundation board organization and training. STCC's specific need was a format that would enable it to qualify and especially quantify responses from representatives of several area clusters.

The methodology involves both individual answers and group feedback on questions designed to identify ways in which the college's academic programs, career services, and corporate and professional programs could better serve local businesses and agencies. Little said the Clements Group is essentially providing an infrastructure for ongoing assessment. The forums differ from many of the school's advisory boards in that they involve industry leaders, those who are living the present and have insight into the future. In addition to Porten and Cavagnaro, the hospital forum included human resources managers and other administrators from several area providers, including Baystate Health System, the Sisters of Providence Health System, Hartford Hospital, Shriners Hospital, Berkshire Medical Center, Monson Developmental Center, and many others.

The large-manufacturers forum featured representatives from Friendly's, Lenox/American Saw, Savage Arms, Hasbro, Hazen Paper, and others; the small-manufacturers session included such companies as Bassette Printers, Millitech Corp., Kleer Lumber, Package Machinery, Microtest Laboratories, and Sealed Air Corp. Assessing the first few forums, Little and Carberry said they have been informative and valuable, with responses that range from the predicted to the unexpected.

Results: Predicting Future Business Needs

"We heard about a need for more keyboarding skills for nurses," said Carberry. That point reflects the growing use of laptop computers and personal digital assistants by nurses, doctors, and technicians to enter patient information, prescribe medication, chart treatment, and other uses, she said, adding that it was one of many topics raised during the forum. Porten told BusinessWest that he found the roundtable for hospital administrators to be a worthwhile exercise—one that provided organizers some material for discussion. He said the general focus was on the future of health care, the specific needs of providers, and gaps in training and education that could be filled. There was considerable discussion about the ongoing nursing shortage, he said, adding that he also referenced a looming physician shortage, which may have even more dire consequences for the state's hospitals.

Porten told forum organizers that he would like to see more focus, in general, on clinical decision making in the training of nurses and technicians. He told *Business West* that the medical center puts such employees though a training session—lasting 1 to 3 months—before they can actually see a patient and administer care. With more clinical experience at the college level, he said, Holyoke and other hospitals that have similar regimens may be able to reduce that orientation period, thus saving money in the long run.

FOLLOW-UP

The input from Porten and the others at the hospital forum is being digested, said Carberry, adding that a preliminary report will be sent to attendees. "It will say, in essence, 'this is what we thought we heard you say'," she said, adding that participants will be asked to corroborate those findings and offer additional input. The gathered thoughts and follow-up will eventually shape a final report. When reports from other clusters are completed, the college will then move on to the next step—establishing priorities and crafting responses. Other forums are scheduled for the next several months, she said, and they include the financial services sector, transportation, and K–12 education.

Carberry told *Business West* that if STCC expects to win some of the federal money to be made available to community colleges for workforce development initiatives, it will need both data and partners. The ongoing project is designed to provide both. "This process will enable us to be more proactive, rather than reactive to the needs of businesses," she explained. "We've seen a ton of energy come out of the first forums … we want to take that energy and use it to strengthen all these clusters."

Note. From "Building business partnerships," 2005, *Business West, 21*(13), p. 10. Copyright 2005 by *Business West.* Adapted with permission.

CASE *21*

Housatonic Community College Brings Employees and Businesses Together

The Business Times

Jobs are the social glue that hold communities together. This case study describes how one community college helps train individuals to meet employers' needs for entry-level talent.

Housatonic Community College (HCC), Bridgeport, Connecticut, which attracted attention in early 2002 with its business partnership program, is starting a business program that will bring new employees to businesses free-of-charge. HCC will launch a cooperative education program to provide employers with qualified students for paid internships and other full- and part-time positions. According to Cooperative Education Coordinator Marie Geelan, interns and part-time students can become a pool of trained, skilled candidates to be considered when full-time openings occur. "Having access to such temporary workers can take the guesswork out of the hiring process," said Geelan. "No longer will businesses have to take a chance on a stranger when filling vacancies; they can draw from a pool of students whose knowledge, skills, behavior, and attitudes are known quantities."

The program also can serve as a source of quality, full-time employees who have the skills, education, and workplace values employers want, she said. The co-op program is the latest in a series of programs the college has introduced in an effort to meet the training and education needs of businesses in its 11-town service area. Recent initiatives include the following:

- Creating a partnership with area businesses that resulted in $1.8 million in grants to train workers while providing the area's population, which includes a heavy concentration of African Americans, Latinos, Asian Americans, Native Americans, and recent European immigrants, a ladder into the middle class.
- Adding 22 new associate degree and certificate programs in response to regional and national workplace needs. These programs will enable many students to pursue careers in South Central Connecticut—not on the other side of the country or the globe.
- Playing a lead role in the creation of the Bridgeport Economic Resource Center, the area agency charged with attracting and retaining industry.
- Acting as a catalyst in the creation of an alliance of area metal manufacturers that has taken concrete steps to improve the competitiveness of the area's largest industry.

To participate in the cooperative education program, students must enroll in a three-credit course that will cover such things as the importance of making a good impression; demonstrating a positive attitude; maintaining a good appearance; and relating well with superiors, colleagues, and the public. Geelan added, "This class will enable these students to stand out from others their age."

The teacher training programs at the University of Bridgeport recently received certification from the state board of education. Dean James J. Ritchie of the University of Bridgeport School of Education and Human Resources said the state approvals are recognition of the quality of the program. "A lot of people at [the University of Bridgeport] have worked hard for this," he said. University President Neil A. Salonen said the approvals are an affirmation of the "commitment [the University of Bridgeport] has made to building an academic program recognized for its excellence."

The state approvals allow the University of Bridgeport to certify students to teach subjects at various grade levels. They also mark a major turnaround for the school of education that, before Ritchie's appointment in 1998, was in danger of losing approvals for its teacher training programs. The state gave 5-year approvals of the University of Bridgeport's secondary and elementary programs, authorizing them through 2006. The state's staff report found that in the secondary and elementary programs and in special subject areas, the program fully met the 49 standards. Five of those standards were met "with distinction," the report said.

The middle grade (grades 4–7) subject certification and the intermediate school administration programs were given 2-year authorizations, through 2003. The state raised some concerns about class scheduling and recordkeeping. According to Ritchie those concerns have been addressed. The state also gave University of Bridgeport approval for preparation programs for teaching general science and for training reading and language arts consultants. The University of Bridgeport graduate school of education has more than 400 students in its programs with courses held at the Bridgeport campus and at satellite facilities in Stamford, Waterbury, and North Haven.

Note. From "Housatonic Community College Brings Employees and Businesses Together," January 1, 2002, *The Business Times, 24*(1), p. 10. Copyright 2005 by New Haven Business Times. Adapted with permission.

CASE 22

Local Demand Should Drive Community College Efforts

Vocational Training News

How should community college career and technical education programs respond to community needs? This case study illustrates how knowledge of the local labor market helps community colleges ensure that they are properly positioned as a step in career pathways.

Successful career and technical education programs at community colleges are driven by the demands of local markets and lead students to credentials that make them instantly employable, according to an official at a 2-year college. "It is important for community colleges to know as much as possible about the communities and labor markets that their students face," said James Jacobs, director of the Center for Workforce Development and Policy at Macomb Community College in Warren, Michigan. "Without properly assessing the demands of the private sector, it's difficult to offer programming that meets students' needs," he added.

"Collaboration, whether between 2-year colleges and employers or the K–12 system, community colleges, and 4-year schools, is also vital if a technical education program is to accomplish its mission," Jacobs said at the National Dissemination Center for Career and Technical Education at The Ohio State University in Columbus. "Normally, to make a program work—and work well—one institution doesn't have all the answers or all the resources," he said. Specifically, Jacobs cited nursing and information technology as fields that have commonly incorporated effective practices into their certificate programs.

Also, institutions have used National Science Foundation (NSF) Advanced Technology Education grants to create effective programs. "Many of these colleges that have developed programming [with the NSF funding] have come out with extremely interesting programs that get students good jobs and are based on an intensive use of science and math curricula," said Jacobs, who is also the associate director for community college operations at the Community College Research Center.

In addition, Jacobs recommended that vocational education programs at 2-year institutions partner and align themselves with public workforce efforts, including state and local Workforce Investment Act and Temporary Assistance to Needy Families programs. "The main focus [of career education programs]—where the rubber meets the road ... is its emphasis on workforce development," he said. "And there's a substantial connection between what community colleges do in their programming and state economic development and workforce development policies."

However, good programs also have a strong institutional support system that can handle all aspects of community college life, including hiring successful instructors, administering financial aid, and offering students remedial classes. In reality, classroom activity is less than half of the story, stressed Jacobs. Jacobs noted that there is a "new landscape," with community college career and technical education programs often viewed as a step in career pathways to fields that require 4-year degrees, such as engineering.

Although approximately 85% of postsecondary Carl D. Perkins Vocational and Technical Education Act dollars are currently concentrated in community colleges, Jacobs warned the money provided by the federal program is not sufficient to meet all their needs. Community colleges should use Perkins funding to complement their program's focus, not define it.

Note. From "Local Demand Should Drive Community College Efforts," 2003, *Vocational Training News, 34*(10), p. 8. Copyright 2003 by LRP Publications. Adapted with permission.

PART 5

Case Studies of Community Colleges Supporting Economic Development

The role of community colleges in economic development is perhaps not as widely understood as it should be by many public officials and members of the public. The cases in this section focus on that role.

Case 23. Transformation of an Organization to a Lean Enterprise: Economic Development Implications

Case 24. Johnson County Community College and Burlington Northern Santa Fe Railroad Form a Unique Partnership

Case 25. Colorado Community Colleges: Full Partners in Economic Development

Case 26. From Swords to Suppliers: The Role of a Community College in Defense Conversion

Case 27. World-Class Training Center Helps South Carolina Companies Compete Globally

Case 28. Community College of Southern Nevada Looks to Spur Economic Growth

CASE 23

Transformation of an Organization to a Lean Enterprise: Economic Development Implications

John F. Blasdell and John D. Piccolo

*A traditional problem in the United States is that workforce
developers and economic developers do not always communicate
as effectively as they should. Community colleges can and do
play an important role in meeting local economic
development needs, as this case documents.*

Since 1919, the Triangle company name has been synonymous with steel leaf springs used in the transportation industry. Triangle Springs was originally located in the vibrant Golden Triangle section of Pittsburgh, Pennsylvania—hence its name. Fortunately for the area, the original owner of the company had a vacation home in DuBois, Pennsylvania, and decided in 1927 to relocate the company to DuBois, a small town situated in north-central Pennsylvania.

Triangle Suspension Systems (TSS) is a midsized company of approximately 230 employees, with 135 employed in manufacturing and 95 employed in distribution. The manufacturing division of the company produces standard multileaf springs and state-of-the-art parabolic springs. Although 75% of its production is standard multileaf springs, the company will be producing more parabolic springs in the future, because 90% of Class A vehicles on the road have them on their front and rear axles. The distribution division of TSS sells a full line of brake and suspension components to the heavy truck independent after market. The organization distributes brand names such as Triangle Springs, Flagg Suspension Parts, Triangle Air Spring, Leland Brake & Wheel Parts, and TMR Spring Brakes. Some customers include Fleet Pride and Inland Truck Parts, along with 200 independent service repair facilities. Currently, TSS is a highly efficient, profitable, midsized company that is firmly entrenched in the local community. Arguably, the most significant event that has contributed to the organization's present status is participation in lean manufacturing training in 2003.

NEED FOR CHANGE

According to Bob Heberling, director of lean manufacturing for TSS, the organization began working on continuous improvement programs in 1995. Some of the indicators that drove the change initiative included unsatisfactory lead time, unsatisfactory quality, waste, bottlenecks, on-time delivery problems, and a resultant decline in business. To address these issues, Triangle began by moving to a team-based organization in which strategic project management teams were organized to address continuous improvement initiatives. Many of the changes were based on lean principles, such as cellular manufacturing and set-up reduction. Interestingly, the initiatives were not formally known as lean manufacturing.

This approach was consistent with that of many U.S. companies in the mid- to late 1990s that tried to implement various components of lean manufacturing instead of approaching it as a business philosophy. Triangle had been a batch manufacturing facility for many years with varying degrees of success. As a result, many of the older managers became extremely comfortable and resisted change. Despite the barrier to change, the organization did make some significant gains during this period. Manufacturing lead time was cut from 14 weeks to 6 weeks and then to 4 weeks; cycle time was reduced from 20 days to 5 days; production hours per ton improved from 30 to 16.

Because of leadership change, the continuous improvement initiatives lost a bit of momentum until 2002, when Triangle initiated "Kaizen" events. Kaizen is a Japanese term meaning improvement (Kotelnikov, n.d.). Kaizen teams formally analyzed a process and made improvements. Eager to expand on the gains made with Kaizen events, the leadership at Triangle started looking for a more comprehensive, formalized approach to process improvement. Senior management began to read newspaper and journal articles on how other organizations developed success by implementing lean manufacturing. During this period, a stakeholder from the organization submitted a brochure to Nancy Plows, the human resource manager, regarding lean manufacturing public workshops offerings in the area through the collaborative efforts of Pennsylvania State University-DuBois and the Northwest Pennsylvania Industrial Resource Center (NWIRC) in Erie. A meeting was subsequently arranged with the Triangle's leadership team to present an overview of the program series and to review the content of the curriculum and the inherent benefits of the program. The organization decided it would be better suited to undertake the lean programming through a contract training venue, in which the program would be delivered exclusively to TSS. This strategy would allow for customization and scheduling to suit company needs.

What Is Lean Manufacturing?

Lean manufacturing is a common-sense business philosophy geared toward eliminating non–value-added activity throughout an organization. Lean manufacturing uses cross-functional teams and a systematic approach to continuous improvement. It allows organizations to make remarkable improvements in efficiency, profitability, and customer satisfaction.

Henry Ford was actually the first true lean thinker, with the development of his continuous flow assembly plant at Highland Park. Unfortunately, the system was not designed to accommodate changeovers. Ford mistakenly assumed that people would always be content with the same style and color of cars, which meant that every machine was built to manufacture a specific part number. It was this assumption and the fact that he did not have a good total productive maintenance (TPM) system that ultimately led Ford to rearrange his machinery into production departments (Womack, Jones, & Roos, 1990).

It was not until after World War II that Taichi Ohno of Toyota in Japan started to develop true lean manufacturing principles. Like many organizations that develop into a lean enterprise, it was done out of sheer necessity. Toyota had neither the space nor the resources to hold inventory. Faced with a lack of money and space, small market demand, and a need for product diversification, Toyota could not survive using the Ford style of mass production. This quandary marked the beginning of the Toyota Production System, later to be known as lean manufacturing (Womack et al., 1990).

Womack conveyed that in was not until the 1980s, when the "Big Three" automakers started losing significant market share to Japan, that lean manufacturing became prominent in the United States. Unfortunately, many of the U.S. companies just tried to implement components of lean, such as quality circles and statistical process control. It took most U.S.-based companies another 10 years to realize that lean manufacturing is a complete system: a business philosophy that is not just a series of isolated techniques.

Today, lean principles have been widely published and successfully applied at many U.S. companies. Lean lends itself well not only to manufacturing but also to organizations that specialize in service and administration. To this end, organizations are widening the scope and focus of lean manufacturing to include all processes that impact the bottom line. More and more organizations are becoming customer centered in their approach to the market, which goes hand in hand with the principles of lean manufacturing. To meet customer demands, organizations not only have to focus on taking out non–value-added processes but also need to ensure that they know exactly what their customer wants and when they want it. With this in mind, the lean philosophy is now being applied to all areas within an organization—from production to sales and engineering. It is finally being recognized that the true benefits of lean thinking will only be fully realized when the entire organization embraces the philosophy.

In describing lean manufacturing, it is important to emphasize what lean is not. Lean is not a way to reduce the workforce. Organizations that use any continuous improvement program to reduce the workforce will eventually find themselves dealing with a lack of cooperation from the only true resource that makes such a program successful: its people. Management must make it clear from the beginning that people will not lose jobs; rather they may be moved laterally or promoted to help support new or existing programs as a result of lean implementation. This point cannot be stressed enough. It is crucial to the long-term success of any program that the workforce not be adversely affected on the implementation of lean.

A COLLABORATIVE EFFORT

The program delivery of lean manufacturing to TSS is the result of a collaborative effort between Penn State DuBois and NWIRC. The partnership forged between Penn State DuBois and NWIRC is unique in Pennsylvania and serves as a model for collaboration between an educational institution and an economic development entity. The mission of the professional development component at Penn State DuBois Continuing Education is to help clients solve problems through quality education and training. Inherent to this mission is the promotion of the concept that education and training must be strategic and proactive to obtain maximum benefit.

NWIRC is a private, nonprofit economic development corporation working to improve the competitiveness of small- and medium-sized manufacturers in the northwest and north central Pennsylvania regions. NWIRC is supported by the Commonwealth of Pennsylvania Office of Science Technology and Workforce and the National Institute of Standards and Technology's Manufacturing Extension Partnership. The collaborative relationship between Penn State DuBois and NWIRC is a marriage of two programs that previously competed for the same audience. Before the relationship, a competitive model existed in the north central Pennsylvania region between the two entities, with both vying for the same market. This resulted in lean manufacturing programs being canceled at the expense of everyone involved. This was creating a gap in delivering this knowledge to organizations.

In 2001, instead of competing, a plan to collaborate was formulated to capitalize on the best that both entities had to offer. This collaboration created a synergy that resulted in increased market penetration, both in public workshop and contract training venues. In turn, a significant transfer of knowledge relative to lean manufacturing occurred in the region. In fact, over the last 3 years approximately 1,185 participants haven enrolled in some form of lean manufacturing, representing 44 organizations.

One of the key elements associated with the success of this partnership is the instructional capabilities of Howard Wilson. Wilson is currently an applications engineer with NWIRC. He has a bachelor of science degree in mechanical engineering and a master of engineering degree from Penn State. He has taught mechanical design and industrial management at Penn State Erie and Gannon University. His industrial experience includes mechanical design, product development, and process improvement. Wilson has both the theoretical and practical background essential to delivering this type of training in a real world environment.

Lean manufacturing training and implementation has resulted in increasing the manufacturing efficiencies of organizations in north central Pennsylvania. The Triangle story is just one of many untold stories throughout this area by organizations that have benefited from this model to access lean manufacturing training.

PROGRAM DELIVERY

Management at TSS decided to offer the full lean manufacturing series initially to 14 critical stakeholders within the organization. The curriculum was developed by the NIST Manufacturing Extension Partnership and contains a perfect blend of classroom instruction and live simulation. The full program consists of seven modules totaling 49 hours (4.9 continuing education units). On successful completion of the programming, each participant receives a lean manufacturing certificate. Given the financial status of the organization at the time, the financial outlay for this program was substantial. The programming commenced on February 3, 2003, and ended on March 24, 2003. The following is a brief description of the lean manufacturing modules:

- Lean 101—Introduction to Lean Manufacturing. This 8-hour program is a mixture of lecture and hands-on live simulation, teaching lessons in standardized work, workplace organization, visual controls, set-up reduction, batch size reduction, point of use storage, quality at the source, workforce practices, and pull systems, each designed to eliminate waste in the manufacturing process. This is a recommended prerequisite for the remaining lean manufacturing programs.
- Lean 202—Value Stream Mapping. This 4-hour program illustrates how to map the current state of a product or process with current data and non–value-added processes and then map the future state. Participants learn the steps necessary to eliminate waste in the system via the power of a value stream map to achieve the enhanced future state. Real company examples and case studies are presented.
- Lean 203—5S (Visual) Workplace Organization and Standardization. This is an 8-hour program that allows participants the opportunity to experience first-hand how the 5S System reduces waste in the mounting plate assembly area of a simulated production facility. Participants learn the concepts of the 5S

system and then apply them to transform a dirty, disorganized production area into a clean, organized, and orderly workplace.

- Lean 204—Set-Up Reduction. This 7-hour program clearly defines set-up and discusses reasons and barriers to reducing set-up time. The course follows the principles first expressed by Shigeo Shingo and his work on Single Minute Exchange of Dies (SMED). Participants learn the standard methodology in applying SMED to any type of setup or industry.
- Lean 205—Cellular/Flow Manufacturing. This 7-hour program illustrates the five-step process for designing and implementing work cells, focusing on reduced lead times, minimizing work in process, optimizing floor space usage, and improving productivity. The process applies to both assembly and machining applications.
- Lean 206—Pull Systems/Kanban. This 8-hour program demonstrates the power of implementing a pull system in a manufacturing operation. Participants take part in manufacturing simulations that compare push-and-pull systems and then design a pull system for a case study factory. The course includes three case studies that show results that various manufacturers have achieved with pull.
- Lean 207—Total Productive Maintenance (TPM). This 7-hour program conveys the fundamental principles of TPM. The participants will learn to proactively maintain machines and equipment at their peak productivity. Participants will gain a basic understanding of TPM and its five major components, which cover maintenance prevention, preventative maintenance, and improvement-related maintenance.

An element fundamental to the success of lean manufacturing implementation at TSS was the application of the lean concepts and principles learned during the course of the training. According to the vice president, Harry Pehote, the stakeholders periodically met during the training to discuss implementation strategies. The application of lean concepts to the shop floor was critical to the organization's becoming a lean enterprise.

BENEFITS

A multitude of benefits, both qualitative and quantitative, resulted from the lean manufacturing training. Some were anticipated, and others were not. Accidents dropped drastically at TSS. Plows (the human resource manager) attributed this to 5S implementation that deals with workplace standardization, organization, and cleanliness. This is not unusual. According to instructor Wilson, oftentimes organizations will see a decrease in accidents because of 5S implementation, and some organizations actually identify safety as an "S" in their 5S program.

According to Plows, lean manufacturing training transferred abstract concepts to a formalized, disciplined approach for fixing problems. It also introduced standard terminology for the manufacturing operation. Plows went on to state that the organization "knew the tools but had to put them all together." Plows' reaction may have resulted from the remnants of implementing some lean concepts in the early 1990s. The training essentially allowed the Triangle organization to look at lean manufacturing as a philosophy.

Lean manufacturing concepts were able to be seamlessly integrated into the 80/20 corporate philosophy of The Marmon Group. According to Pehote, the underlying principle of this philosophy is that 80% of business sales are derived from 20% of its customers. Within a larger context, this way of doing business simplifies and eliminates anything that does not add value. Heberling conveyed that because both of these philosophies involve the elimination of non–value-added activity, they fit nicely with each other.

As the lean manufacturing process was implemented, the organization was inundated with suggestions for improvement from front-line workers. Previously, this was not a regular occurrence in the Triangle organization. Employees began to realize that they were empowered to make improvements to the organization. This sense of ownership is a positive outcome in a lean enterprise. The indicators or measures that TSS uses to determine success improved substantially.

Table 23.1	Impact of Lean Training on Organizational Metrics	
Metrics	**Before Lean Training**	**After Lean Training**
Cost/ton of steel	$1,400.00	$800.00
Cycle time	8.5 days	5 days
Person hours/spring	0.5 hours	0.45 hours

As the Table 23.1 illustrates, there were improvements with each of the indicators. Work in process (WIP) reduction that is actually reflected in the cycle time metric translates into reduced inventory and increased cash flow. These improvements have resulted in increased efficiencies for the Triangle organization. Heberling cautioned, however, that the organization has "just scratched the surface" in relation to the potential for more improvements.

The improved efficiencies previously documented have increased the profitability of TSS. Although the organization would not comment on profit margin increases, there are certain activities that would point to their significance. For example, employees are participating in a healthy profit-sharing plan. Pehote stated that at one point, instead of planning for the future of Triangle, the organization was contemplating severance packages.

TSS has experienced a surge in business, primarily because it was able to improve efficiencies and reduce costs through lean manufacturing. According to Pehote, a number of factors contributed to the upswing in business. Although lean manufacturing training and implementation was a significant factor, other factors are important to relate. Pehote explained that between 1997 and 2000, there were more trucks produced than the previous 10 years. Because new trucks usually do not require parts, the business was in a downward spiral. However, as the trucks on the road are getting older, they are requiring after-market parts. In addition, 9 tons of production was obtained from a facility in Cambridge, Ontario, that was closed because of overcapacity in Canada. DuBois is now serving the Canadian market.

Perhaps the most compelling reason for the surge in business is the reverse outsourcing of the after-market business from Monterrey, Mexico. According to Pehote, the DuBois facility was able to produce more efficiently and cheaper despite the fact that labor at the Monterrey plant was one-third the cost of labor in DuBois. The DuBois facility actually became three to four times more productive per person hour than the Mexican facility. This may be the most significant aspect to this success story as many organizations are developing a concession mentality to outsourcing because of low wages paid in other countries. Pehote quipped, "We beat them at their own game."

TSS has added 38 new jobs to the facility since the spring of 2003. This has resulted in an additional $1.8 million pumped back into the local economy. The amount does not consider the ripple effect of these wages. Marmon Highway Technologies is planning to commit $8 million to TSS to construct a new manufacturing facility in DuBois. Lean manufacturing training can be associated with creating a chain of impact that resulted in planning to fund this significant business venture. The construction of this facility will potentially have a positive local economic impact because the organization is committed to using local contractors.

Lean manufacturing principles, in particular, value stream mapping, are being used quite extensively in planning the new facility. Pehote stated that in an environment before lean manufacturing, the stakeholders would have addressed the design of the new facility based on different perspectives. Now, the design of the facility will be based on the lean manufacturing philosophy. With this opportunity, Triangle has the capability to design one of the most efficient facilities of its kind in North America.

TSS has become an important benefactor in the community. A case in point is the commitment of $25,000 to the DuBois Educational Foundation Workforce Development and Technology Center on the Penn State DuBois campus. According to Plows, the benefactor role that Triangle is now able to play would not have been possible without the improvements and efficiencies that lean manufacturing created.

SUMMARY

This case study illustrates a positive chain of impact created by the initial commitment of TSS to address the workforce development needs of 14 critical stakeholders through lean manufacturing training. The lean manufacturing training was offered through a partnership between Penn State DuBois Continuing Education and the Northwest Pennsylvania Industrial Resource Center, consisting of seven courses totaling 49 hours.

The effect of the training was impressive—including a reduction in accidents, reverse outsourcing of jobs from Mexico, and a planned commitment from the parent company of Triangle Suspension System to construct a new $8 million manufacturing facility. The increase in employment and the construction of the new facility will have positive economic development implications.

Critical to the success of the training was the application of the lean concepts and principles learned during the program. Although this should be an obvious transition from learning, many organizations do not get to the application stage. When this occurs, training is devalued in an organization. Therefore, it is incumbent on workforce development professionals to encourage organizations to create a plan to apply learning. This plan ultimately will affect business results. As organizations come to the realization that training can affect business results, it will be easier for it to become part of their organizational culture.

We believe the Triangle story will give other organizations hope and encouragement for competing in a global economy. It is still quite realistic for manufacturers in the United States to thrive if workforce development activities, such as lean manufacturing training, are implemented and applied. At the end of our interview with Triangle in preparation for writing this case study, Pehote, said "Lean put it all together for us." This is a short but powerful statement that provides a lesson in how critical workforce development is for organizations striving to become better and ultimately affecting the economic climate of communities.

References

Kotelnikov, V. (n.d.). *Kaizen*. Retrieved January 20, 2005, from www.1000ventures.com/business_guide/mgmt_kaizen_main.html

Womack, J. P., Jones, D. T., & Roos, D. (1990). *The machine that changed the world*. New York: Macmillan Publishing Company.

CASE 24

Johnson County Community College and Burlington Northern Santa Fe Railroad Form a Unique Partnership

Dan Radakovich

Jobs are key to economic development. This case study describes how one community college contributed to local economic development through a unique partnership with a local employer.

I n 1988, Burlington Northern Railroad (now BNSF—the Burlington Northern Santa Fe Railroad) located its national training headquarters on the campus of the Johnson County Community College (JCCC) in Overland Park, Kansas, which is part of the Greater Kansas City metropolitan area. Although it appears natural to assume that special education developments would come from the relationship with BNSF, the real purpose of the original partnership for JCCC was to encourage local economic development and to provide a new, non-tax revenue stream for the college. The BSNF training center, located on the college campus, now adds more than $60 million annually to the area's community.

JOHNSON COUNTY COMMUNITY COLLEGE AND LOCAL ECONOMIC DEVELOPMENT

Every community college in the nation advocates enhancing local economic development as one of its missions, and nearly all community colleges contribute substantially to the economic well-being of their respective communities. The economic impact of having a community college in a municipality has been well documented in various impact studies and often has been used as a rationale for building a community college in the first place. JCCC's own study shows that JCCC has had an economic impact of far more than $200 million in the community.

In the Kansas City vicinity, community college presidents serve on local chamber councils, and community college personnel are often part of the economic development teams used by communities to sway business and industry to locate in the area. A few local community colleges, however, have gone beyond being community partners in economic development. They have generated substantial economic development initiatives on their own. JCCC, for example, has done just that by forging a partnership with the BNSF Railroad, and the model is one that can be replicated across the country.

Charles J. Carlsen, president of JCCC, was instrumental in creating the partnership. He has always held that economic development is one of the main missions of a good community college, and this commitment led him to establish the Johnson County Business and Industry Institute at the JCCC campus in 1984. He gave the institute these operating goals:

- Serve the educational needs of business and industry in Johnson County.
- Generate revenues to offset the direct cost of the partnership and generate revenue that can be used to further assist the college.
- Promote economic development in Johnson County by cooperating with involved county governments and municipal chambers of commerce.

THE PARTNERSHIP AND THE PLAN

The partnership with BNSF evolved because of the JCCC Business and Industry Institute's commitment to explore all economic development initiatives on behalf of JCCC. The BNSF Railroad is one of this nation's largest railroads and is an innovative leader in the industry. In 1985, the then Burlington Northern Railroad operated a 14,000-square-foot training facility in the Argentine district of Kansas City, Kansas, near the rail yards. Mike Voelker, former BNSF director of technical training, learned of the services of the JCCC Business and Industry Institute and commissioned JCCC's Office of Institutional Research to assist him in designing needs assessments for several courses he was developing for electricians and welders. As the relationship between BNSF and JCCC developed, BNSF announced plans to build a larger training facility. Preliminary discussion about locating the center on the JCCC campus (approximately 1 mile west of the BNSF regional corporate offices) was started by Don Doucette, former JCCC director of institutional research; Don Goldenbaum, former director of the business and industry institute at JCCC; and Mike Voelker.

The new facility had to be flexible, cost-efficient, and considerably larger than BNSF's Kansas City operation. Voelker was looking for a good environment for students and staff—a facility conducive to learning, as well as a facility with some attractive financing. The railroad had looked at sites in Dallas, Spokane, and Fort Worth, as well as Kansas City. The idea of having a training facility on a college campus, however, appealed to BNSF's Voelker, and the college and BNSF began to discuss the feasibility of locating the BNSF center on the JCCC campus.

Originally, BNSF wanted JCCC to build the facility and then lease space to BNSF. However, the college was advised that it would lose its tax-exempt status if that were done, and also that the deal would probably alienate every developer in Johnson County in the process. The college asked BNSF to build the facility and then donate it to the college; the railroad did not want to do that. Still, the idea of a partnership was so appealing that the two sides continued to pursue options.

Finally, BNSF and JCCC personnel approached the city of Overland Park about the possibility of issuing industrial revenue bonds to finance the building. They were not optimistic, because the city had been reluctant to issue bonds in the past. Because of the unique request, however, the city of Overland Park felt that, because no industrial competitive advantage was being offered, the issuance of bonds to BNSF might very likely create a great deal of economic development for Overland Park and Johnson County.

The city thus approved $2.9 million in revenue bonds. The partnership between the city of Overland Park, JCCC, and BNSF Railroad called for a 52,000-square-foot facility to be built on the JCCC campus. BNSF was to pay off the bonds over a 10-year period, subleasing approximately one third of the space to the college at cost. After 10 years, when the building was paid off, BNSF would donate it to JCCC. BNSF would then be able to lease the building for three 5-year periods after the college took possession. As a result, the Industrial Technical Center was constructed. It was occupied in January 1988. In June 1991, the partners agreed to double the size of the center, dividing construction costs as they had before.

Although numerous educational developments would accrue to JCCC from its association with BNSF, JCCC's primary purpose was to encourage local economic development and to provide new nontax revenue for the college. BNSF wanted high-quality teaching space—a real "educational" atmosphere—to train its staff at the most reasonable cost to the corporation. JCCC understood the economic development opportunities for the Johnson County area and for the college and hoped that future educational partnerships would develop. Nonetheless, the JCCC–BNSF partnership caused a lot of concern on the JCCC campus, particularly among faculty. Some faculty wondered why the college should concern itself with county economic development at the expense of direct training. But the president's vision prevailed; the center was built.

FUNDING THE COOPERATIVE

As the partnership has grown, the two sides have adopted various agreements for funding the cooperative. Fixed quarterly and semiannual expenses were paid by

BNSF and reimbursed by JCCC. Initial construction was financed by 10-year industrial revenue bonds issued by the city of Overland Park. BNSF made quarterly payments to the city to retire the bonds, and JCCC makes quarterly payments to reimburse BNSF for its share: 36% of the initial building. Payments were made semiannually. Initial construction bonds were issued in December 1986 and retired in December 1996. Ownership of the initial building then reverted to JCCC, although BNSF leased training space at a much-reduced fee (less than $5/square foot) for three additional 5-year terms, the first beginning in December 1996, the second in December 2001, and the third in December 2006. Construction bonds for the expansion of the building were issued in June 1991 and were retired in June 2001. BNSF made semiannual payments to the city and was reimbursed by JCCC for its 45% share. As with the initial building, after the bonds were retired, ownership of the expanded space reverted to JCCC. BNSF may lease it from JCCC at a fee to be determined for three additional 5-year terms.

Fixed monthly expenses were billed by JCCC and paid by BNSF. JCCC and BNSF divide operating costs—including costs for utilities, janitorial services, sewer, repairs, and maintenance—according to percentages of building use, as measured in square feet: for the initial building, 64% BNSF/36% JCCC; for the expansion, 52% BNSF/48% JCCC. JCCC assigned a fee per square foot by comparing the previous year's operating expenses to the percentages of space used by each party. JCCC maintained public liability insurance on the ITC, and BNSF and JCCC separately insured their own furnishings and equipment. The city of Overland Park required that BNSF and JCCC maintain fire, casualty, and property insurance on the ITC—in proportion to their ownership—until the bonds were retired.

INSTRUCTIONAL DESIGN AND SUPPORT

BNSF outsources its instructional design to the college, which assigns some instructional design and support staff to BNSF according to its needs. These staff members serve in BNSF's Training Systems Development group. BNSF pays the staff members' salaries and benefits plus 8% to cover JCCC's administrative costs. Other forms of support are as follows.

Cost for credit instruction to JCCC. JCCC has commissioned the National Academy for Railroad Sciences (NARS) to teach selected courses in railroad conducting and railroad dispatching as part of the associate of science degree in railroad operations. JCCC pays NARS the sum of $500 per student week for that training. JCCC expects 11 conductor and 9 dispatcher classes to be offered for an estimated total of 1,880 weeks. At $500 per student week, JCCC could reimburse NARS $940,000 during the academic year. Conductor students are required to pay all of these costs, but dispatcher students may receive scholarships from BNSF.

Student scholarships through the JCCC Foundation. BNSF offers scholarships for students who are enrolled in the dispatcher option of JCCC's associate degree in railroad operations program. These scholarships help students defray the cost of tests and exams, tuition, and fees, as well as some of the costs associated with required off-campus training. The scholarships amount to $7,000 for each dispatcher student.

Gifts and donations from BNSF to JCCC. Other than scholarships, BNSF makes several annual contributions to JCCC. These gifts help to support events at the Cultural Education Center, outstanding faculty awards, and the college's main fundraising affair. These contributions amounted to $21,000 in 1998.

ECONOMIC BENEFIT TO JOHNSON COUNTY

BNSF moved its operation to the JCCC campus in 1988. BNSF brought 3,000 of its employees to the area and commissioned 20,000 room nights from the Doubletree Hotel, one of only two hotels located near the college. The training facility had a full-time staff of 10. BNSF expects to train more than 12,000 employees at the center this year. Those students will comprise 20,500 student weeks of training (number of students times the weeks on campus), which yields 110,000 room nights for the seven local hotels and motels now located near the college. After calculating travel, food costs, and the cost of maintaining the training facility, the economic impact for Johnson County is substantial. The BNSF operating budget for this area is more than $25 million. Applying the multiplier of $2.50 for each dollar spent in the area, the economic benefit to the area will exceed $60 million per year.

CREDIT INSTRUCTION

The first credit courses offered as part of the partnership with BNSF were in track welding. JCCC assisted BNSF in course development and competency assessment as part of the original contract. When BNSF moved to the campus, the college began to offer track welding on campus. However, because track welding is somewhat unique, BNSF first sent college staff into the field to learn more about that process. The college then offered credit instruction for BNSF in electronics, hydraulics, pneumatics, and construction and bridge repair. The electronics program was developed so that students could do most of their work at home. Students came to the JCCC campus for 6 weeks over an 18-month period and did the rest of the work from their home computers. Students communicated daily with their instructors via modems. Fifteen people from all over the country have completed the degree requirements for the electronics program.

ASSOCIATE DEGREE IN RAILROADING

As BNSF's business grew, it had to expand its workforce to keep pace with demand. The college had always wanted an entry into railroading. Thus, the college approached BNSF's director, Ed Butt, about the possibility of working together to offer a program. He was supportive of a joint venture between the college and the railroad to expand the opportunity for railroad training and retraining and to initiate the world's first associate degree program in railroad occupations. With Butt's support, JCCC and BNSF initiated a national center for railroad training and education. This center, the National Academy of Railroad Science (NARS), provides the training stipulated in the Rail Safety Improvement Act of 1988 for engineer certification. In addition, NARS offers training in right-of-way maintenance, train conducting, communications and customer service, signal training, dispatcher training, and mechanical training for machinists, electricians, and car men.

BNSF took the lead and has allowed the college to offer certificate and degree programs in dispatcher training, conductor training, and right-of-way maintenance. However, the college and BNSF did not stop there. They recognized the need for a wider distribution (this is a national program) to prepare people for positions with the nation's railroads. The associate degree in railroading is a 2-year associate of science or associate of applied science degree that prepares graduates for careers in railroad operations (customer service, conductor and yard crews, dispatching, locomotive engineer, right-of-way maintenance, mechanical, signal systems, system electrical, and telecommunications). The degrees are offered by a consortium of community and technical colleges and universities to produce a pool of graduates from which all railroads can hire. In addition, the degree programs offer railroad employees opportunities to broaden and update their skills even if they do not want degrees.

IMPACT AND REFLECTIONS

The national attention that the JCCC/BNSF Railroad partnership has been given is phenomenal: Not a week has gone by without some kind of inquiry or visit. The program was recognized by the American Association of Community Colleges as one of the nation's best. In April 1995, the program gained yet more kudos when then-Secretary of Labor Robert Reich called it a model of cooperation between education and industry. America's success in meeting the challenges of uncertain but far-reaching change will depend on how public and private sectors work together to guarantee a workforce that is skilled and productive. The relationship between JCCC and BNSF has demonstrated that and more, and this relationship may even be the catalyst for establishing competency criteria for employment in the nation's railroads.

The impact on local economic development—more than $60 million a year— is substantial. Yet, surprisingly, of all the good things associated with the cooperation, this economic impact is often taken for granted or ignored altogether. Some people still view this partnership negatively by claiming that it is a taxpayer subsidy to the railroad industry. They forget that all new construction will eventually become the property of JCCC. Conversely, BNSF sometimes gets the sense that it is dealing with a college looking for a handout.

Many myths are associated with any public–private partnership. One of the biggest is that the company has unlimited funds and that it will be willing to support any and all college projects. In truth, the company seeks the best return on its investment, and cost is always a factor. Another myth suggests that unlimited grants will be available to support the public–private venture, particularly if jobs are promised. In reality, only a few opportunities exist for outside support of partnership ventures.

One final myth suggests that all people will appreciate efforts to enhance colleges by working closely with corporations or to enhance corporate training by working closely with colleges. Some people at JCCC, for example, still fear that the college has become "Choo Choo U," and they suggest that the tail (the BNSF program) is wagging the dog. Many at BNSF question any attempt to change traditional hiring practices. Some are threatened by tying employment to education, maintaining that training must be done on the job.

CONCLUSION

The future holds great promise for cooperative efforts between colleges and industries. Colleges and corporations have been creating partnerships for a long time. People have debunked the myths, and they know that a true partnership has to be productive for both entities and that it must be cost-effective as well. Hard work, not wishful thinking, is the key to successful partnerships.

Private industry and public education must work together to allow increasing numbers of people to move into the economic mainstream of American life through employment tied to training. Colleges and corporations can make that happen more effectively by working together rather than by working separately. The partnership between BNSF Railroad and JCCC is, indeed, an exemplary model. The economic benefit to BNSF employees and new students is obvious, and the benefit to the nation's railroads will be felt for years to come. The economic benefit for Johnson County, Kansas, continues to expand year after year.

Note. From "Johnson County Community College, Burlington Northern Santa Fe Railroad Form Unique Partnership," by D. Radakovich, 1998, *Economic Development Review, 15*(4), pp. 22–25. Copyright 1998 by American Economic Development Council. Adapted with permission.

CASE 25

Colorado Community Colleges: Full Partners in Economic Development

Jim L. Raughton

This case describes an initiative in Colorado that shows how one state positioned community colleges to serve a more effective role in economic development.

In May 1985, Richard D. Lamm, then-Governor of Colorado, signed House Bill 1187, which reconfigured the relationship between the State Board for Community Colleges and Occupational Education and the member community colleges. The bill gave new authority to the state board, allowing it to appoint college presidents and to create a vision for the role of community colleges within Colorado's educational system. This legislation created a framework for a new culture within Colorado's community colleges.

Before this legislation, each college fulfilled its academic mission in relative isolation and with considerable autonomy. This situation made it difficult for the community college system as a whole to exert influence or to have much impact on larger issues, including regional economic development. The state board's new authority changed all that. In 1986, the board used its expanded authority to introduce dramatic changes to the way the community college system was governed. In a bold and controversial move, the board radically restructured the system to a degree that was unique in the nation so that community colleges would be better equipped to become full partners in area economic development.

The board's first step was to select someone to help guide the restructuring of the 20-year-old system. The board selected Jerome F. Wartgow as president of the new community college system—a title that combined the positions of director of community colleges and director of vocational education. The board gave Wartgow a mandate to reshape, consolidate, and restructure the colleges into the largest postsecondary educational system in Colorado.

This reorganization brought with it a set of unexpected challenges. Community colleges in Colorado, like many community colleges throughout the nation, were widely perceived to be the least important of the state's institutions of higher education. Thus, community colleges were accustomed to a lack of resources, which often kept them from fully participating in the state's economic development initiatives. Therefore, for the new system to fulfill its potential, its leadership had to be able to reward initiative and to reestablish community colleges as important educational institutions. What followed was the creation of a framework for that innovation.

ORGANIZED FOR ECONOMIC DEVELOPMENT

It was also decided that changing the community college culture would require rebuilding a core team of community college presidents and a central administrative staff. The board wanted to create a systemwide organization that encouraged and inspired innovation through competition. The question was how.

The board mandated that the new system should operate with increased "efficiency, accountability, and cost-effectiveness," focusing on people believed to possess vision, drive, and commitment. These people would constitute the management team. Once the team was in place, team members were given the charge to develop an educational system that emphasized the role of community colleges in economic development. After an extensive review, the Colorado Community College and Occupational Education System (CCCOES) was unveiled in 1987 as a merged system that integrated both community college and vocational education curricula. The *Rocky Mountain News* hailed the new system as a "triumph of reform" and praised the state board for streamlining "jury-rigged" institutions. The newspaper expressed hope that the coalition would strengthen both community college and vocational education throughout the state.

ECONOMIC DEVELOPMENT AND COMMUNITY COLLEGE EDUCATION

By 1987, CCCOES had developed a series of educational goals that focused on innovation and excellence. The first of these goals was to ensure that state community colleges provided an undergraduate education that prepared students for meaningful careers. This would include fast-track training and the education of dislocated workers. CCCOES believed that the state could attract new industries if its community colleges produced qualified workers and provided educational leadership in economic development policy. CCCOES determined that the best way to ensure this was to forge a cooperative partnership with other human resource development agencies. The partnership that emerged included a number of agencies, such as the Colorado Office of Business Development, the Governor's Job Training Office, the Department of Labor and Employment, the Department of Rehabilitation Services, the Office of Rural Job Training, local private industry councils, and the Colorado Advanced Technology Institute.

The partnership's goals were simple and straightforward: First, help promote and coordinate state-approved training programs to encourage businesses and industries to locate or expand in Colorado. Second, put resources into programs that displayed a potential for excellence. The partnership also believed that the public was better served if community colleges invested only in fully coordinated economic development initiatives. The partnership sought to clarify the role of the community colleges in the long-term economic future of the state. To emphasize the role of CCCOES in economic development, the State Board for Community Colleges and Occupational Education established an external affairs unit within the CCCOES central office. The purpose of this unit was to identify potential linkages between industry and nontraditional funding sources that could help support new community college educational initiatives.

ECONOMIC DEVELOPMENT SUCCESSES

Since its formation in 1987, CCCOES has accomplished a great deal in its efforts to further economic development in Colorado. In 1994–1995, for example, in cooperation with the Governor's Job Training Office, CCCOES's responsibilities were expanded to include the administration of dislocated workers programs. In addition, the Small Business Administration, based on a proposal developed by CCCOES, began funding small business development centers across the state to support local small businesses. This program has been merged with the Governor's Office of Business Development.

CCCOES programs aimed at fostering economic development have not gone unnoticed. In 1990, CCCOES received the American Association of Community Colleges' Economic Development Award, which honors statewide initiatives built around the concept of partnership. Responding to that award, Colorado's governor, Roy Romer, cited Colorado's community colleges as "major partners in the state's effort to build a top-quality workforce, attract new businesses, and strengthen existing ones."

CCCOES's successes have ensured that community colleges in Colorado will continue to be involved in important policy discussions regarding future economic development. Further, CCCOES, in cooperation with a number of government agencies and business groups, is working to ensure that Colorado's community colleges continue contributing to the state's economic development. As part of that effort, CCCOES—now under the leadership of Dorothy Horrell—is involved in a number of initiatives designed to aid in that mission. These initiatives include the following:

- Colorado FIRST (For Inspiration and Recognition of Science and Technology) and Existing Industry Customized Training Programs
- Accelerated career programs within community colleges
- Telecommunications education
- Workplace learning programs

Colorado recognizes that it must possess a trained workforce if it is to successfully encourage companies to relocate or expand in the state. The Colorado FIRST and Existing Industry Customized Training Programs, which are jointly administered by the Colorado Office of Business Development and CCCOES, are designed to keep Colorado's workforce highly skilled and productive. These programs assist employers in training new or current workers for permanent, non-seasonal jobs. Both programs provide specific job training designed to fit the needs of specific companies. In addition, the programs offer short-term job skill training to unemployed and underemployed Coloradans to enable them to compete for new jobs, thereby reducing the need for public assistance.

Authorized in 1984, the Colorado FIRST Customized Training Program assists basic industry employers with short-term, fast-track training. Since its inception, more than 600 companies of all sizes have used this program, which has provided training for more than 30,000 Coloradans for newly created jobs in manufacturing and business services. For the past 7 years, the customized training programs have operated "payback" models that estimate the time it takes to pay back the state's investment in the training programs. On the basis of current data, in only 1.75 years, Colorado employers will pay back the state's investment in the customized training programs through the taxes generated by the purchasing power of their newly trained employees. Together with other broad-based educational efforts, these programs help create employment opportunities and enhance Colorado's competitive position. In fact, appropriations for these programs have increased continually from $350,000 in 1984 to the present (fiscal year 1998) total of $5.9 million.

ACCELERATED CAREER ACADEMIES

Colorado's community colleges also have created what might be called "accelerated career academies" to help meet the demand for technically trained employees at relocating businesses. These "career academies" are special learning centers set up within various schools in the community college system. They provide adult students with the kind of specific, entry-level job skills actively sought by new employers.

The community college system's most noteworthy career academies include the following:

- The Community College of Denver Technical Education Centers (which focus on fast-track training)
- Red Rocks Community College Business Institute, Lakewood
- Pikes Peak Community College Commerce Centers (which focus on industry-based training), Colorado Springs
- Pueblo Community College Gorsich Advanced Technology Center
- Colorado military base conversion of Lowry Air Force Base to the Higher Education Advanced Technology Center

All of these programs use key features found in all successful fast-track training programs, such as involvement of employers in defining student curricula, on-the-job instruction, and assessment of skills already achieved before entering the educational program.

Through these workforce development programs, state employers and the community college system cooperatively teach current technology and provide job placement opportunities to students. This kind of collaboration between colleges, employers, and students is fundamental to successful statewide economic development. In addition, CCCOES is embracing a wide range of new technologies and using them throughout its system. These technologies include the Internet and related networks as well as public and cable television and satellite networks.

WORKPLACE LEARNING PROGRAMS

To better prepare Colorado students for the opportunities and challenges of tomorrow's workplace, CCCOES, in cooperation with area industries, has developed workplace learning programs. These programs expose students to the demands of the workplace and allow them to see the connection between their academic work and their prospective livelihoods. In the process, students learn tangible skills and develop the kind of critical thinking that adds to their effectiveness and flexibility. Employees also enjoy the benefits of job enrichment and potential career advancement.

Most recently, Colorado's Workplace Learning Project implemented training programs through six participating community colleges and their 14 local business partners. The programs seek the following:

- To provide basic skills to employees to take advantage of continuing employment opportunities, career advancement potential, and improved job performance.
- To develop a program that upgrades the instructional and curriculum development skills of instructors.

- To design a systematic plan of assessment and evaluation that guides the project and provides data for making program improvements.
- To develop a replicable customized basic-skills curricula.
- To disseminate the results of project findings nationally, statewide, and locally.

In addition, Colorado has been awarded a series of three National Workplace Literacy Program grants from the U.S. Department of Education. These grants fund efforts to develop pilot programs in basic workplace skills, to develop a replicable model for training basic-skills instructors, and to design curricula that enhance job skill development. The goal of these efforts is to provide instruction in basic reading, writing, mathematics, and communications skills to workers who are employed in small, medium, and large businesses in urban and rural Colorado communities. The Colorado Literacy Programs should serve as a model for community colleges all across the nation.

CONCLUSION

CCCOES provides students from diverse backgrounds with access to better employment opportunities and a more fulfilling life through education. It is a system that bridges human resource development and economic development to create a culture for innovation in both areas. The CCCOES system offers numerous examples of the kind of fluid, multifaceted role community colleges can play in economic development. Obviously, community colleges can be an important part of the nation's educational system and its vital and diverse economy. The successes of Colorado's community colleges in economic development have created a new perspective on how community colleges can contribute to larger efforts in this area.

Note. From "Colorado Community Colleges: Full Partners in Economic Development," by J. Raughton, 1998, *Economic Development Review, 15*(4), pp. 8–11. Copyright 1998 by American Economic Development Council. Adapted with permission.

CASE 26

From Swords to Suppliers: The Role of a Community College in Defense Conversion

James Jacobs

Many military bases have been closing, which can create hardships for communities and complicate economic development efforts. This case study describes the role played by a Michigan community college to help a local community deal with defense conversion.

Community colleges are well known in economic development circles for customized training. The technical expertise of the faculty, coupled with the flexibility and responsiveness of the institutions, have made these institutions very important to most state training and economic development plans. A 1996 survey of community colleges indicated that more than 93% offered some form of contractual training directed at business and industry. Unfortunately, many people do not fully appreciate the role of community colleges in attracting businesses and other forms of community economic development. Community colleges are committed to working within their communities. In turn, local economic development authorities can use community college resources for surprising, positive, long-term effects.

Macomb Community College (MCC) in Warren, Michigan, upholds this same tradition. When the Detroit Tank Arsenal began to downsize, MCC became involved. Over a 10-year period, it has helped convert the site into a job training facility. MCC's commitment underscores the unique ability of community colleges to marshal an array of resources to aid communities. MCC, like many other community colleges, has played a unique and fundamental role in the economic development of an area beset with serious economic problems.

MILITARY CONVERSION AND ECONOMIC DEVELOPMENT

Although much of the mass media have focused attention on the impact that major military base closings will have on communities, attention also needs to be focused on the substantial impact that defense downsizing has on the U.S. private industrial base, which produces goods and services for the military. A great deal of the U.S. economy has depended on military spending. According to the Congressional Budget Office, for example, 99% of all shipbuilding and 18% of all engineering and scientific instruments were produced for defense applications. It has been estimated that more than 1.8 million private-sector jobs were lost to defense cuts between 1987 and 1997. Thus, any discussion of military spending cutbacks and conversions usually includes two key aspects of economic development: actual base closings and the impact of military contractors shutting down operations.

Actual base closings cost communities numerous jobs, many of them relatively unskilled clerical and service work. Retraining personnel is relatively less difficult than determining the use of the facility after the military leaves. Community colleges have played major roles in many parts of the United States in the development of alternative economic development plans for these facilities. When military contractors shut down operations and lay off thousands of skilled workers, the issue becomes one of the development of alternative economic activities to offset this job loss for communities that have depended on high-wage, high-skilled jobs in their communities. In a period of substantial manufacturing downsizing and loss of jobs to overseas investments, it is often difficult to find economic activity that will easily replace these losses. Again, community colleges can help with economic development alternatives. Both of these economic development issues confronted Macomb County and MCC with the closing of the Detroit Tank Arsenal, a 158-acre military base whose main function was to house a facility where a private contractor, General Dynamics, manufactured the M-1 tank.

MACOMB COUNTY AND THE DETROIT TANK ARSENAL

Macomb County is an industrial suburban area northeast of Detroit, Michigan. More than 730,000 residents live in the 25 suburban communities that comprise the county. What distinguishes Macomb County from stereotypical "suburban bedroom communities" is the dominating presence of auto and auto-related industries. More than 40% of Macomb County's workforce is directly employed in auto manufacturing. When all the industrial services—such as design and engineering service firms—are included, more than two thirds of the workforce is connected to the auto industry. Within Macomb County are not only many of the most important parts and assembly operations of the "Big Three" domestic auto makers but also numerous tool and die shops, machine tool builders, and auto body design firms that provide critical technical talent to the auto industry. Few areas in the United States so completely concentrate their manufacturing in a single industrial product.

The heavy concentration in auto production was the reason the U.S. Army developed the Detroit Tank Arsenal during World War II. The skills needed to build cars and tanks are similar, so the military used people with these skills to build the 1-million-square-foot assembly facility for tanks. For the next 50 years, upwards of 5,000 workers designed, built, and tested a variety of tanks for the Army. Although the land and buildings were part of a secure military base, a civilian subcontractor ran actual productions. Chrysler Corporation hired the workers and administered day-to-day activities, but when Chrysler went through a major restructuring, the business was sold in 1981 to General Dynamics Land Systems. The plant has always been unionized by the United Automobile Workers.

MCC serves 48,000 students: 24,000 in traditional courses and an additional 24,000 in customized training, continuing education, and other activities that relate to the business and labor community. The college operates from three major sites in Macomb County, and it is a major supplier of education and training to the auto and auto-related industry. Macomb maintains the largest apprenticeship and industrial cooperative education program in the state. Its customized training activities generate $15 million in revenue, working with 155 separate companies. In partnership with 21 secondary school districts in the county, MCC has built nationally recognized programs in Tech Prep and School-to-Work.

STAGE ONE: COLLEGE AS TRAINER (RETRAINING AND RECONVERSION)

In the late 1980s, as the military downsizing began, the production of M-1 tanks at the Detroit Arsenal was threatened. For a brief period, the facility was able to find an external market for its products, its major customers being the armed forces of allied countries, primarily in the Middle East. During this period, the workforce continued to shrink. Through the local private industry council, MCC retrained many machinists and operators for work in the private sector. These programs were well received by the plant workers but were often ineffective because the workers who were retrained—many having been placed in new jobs—quickly returned to the plant when any recall was announced as the result of new overseas orders. The high wages at the unionized facility continued to maintain the workforce.

Recognizing this reality, the college, along with the company and the union, decided to pursue a strategy that would attempt to convert the facility into civilian use. In 1993, the college, along with the union and company, participated in writing two grants to the U.S. Department of Defense (DOD) under the Technology Reinvestment Program (TRP). The first grant called for monies to be spent retooling the tank plant to produce an unmanned hazardous environmental control vehicle—the Envirofox. The market for this vehicle was to be private and public fire-fighting units that could dispatch it into fires and environmental spill situations too dangerous for humans. The vehicle contained extensive feedback gauges that could transmit data back to its controllers concerning the extent of a spill's toxicity, thus aiding the vehicle in putting out fires or cleaning up hazardous waste spills.

The second proposal called for the retention of the manufacturing skills of the General Dynamics workers within Macomb County through a retraining process that would convert their skills into those needed by small- and medium-sized manufacturing firms in Macomb County. These firms were expanding and wished to use some of the skills of the General Dynamics workers, such as concurrent engineering. The proposal assumed that upgrading the skills of the former tank plant workers would lead to the growth and development of these firms which, in turn, would lead to the community's retention of high-wage, high-skilled jobs.

Unfortunately, the federal government decided not to fund either proposal. However, in putting together these proposals, the college, union, and company developed a new coalition that would prove useful in the future. Moreover, these initial efforts established an important precedent within the community: that saving the tank plant was less important than retaining high-wage jobs.

Stage Two: College as Planner (Base Closing and Local Reuse)

The next stage in the life of the facility was the announcement in 1995 that DOD intended to close the Detroit Arsenal. This decision meant that the production of tanks finally would be halted permanently, laying off the remaining workers at the facility. In addition, DOD began a conversion process so the City of Warren, Michigan, where the plant was located, could buy the property for use in its economic development. Warren is the largest city in Macomb County. The conversion process called for the city to establish a citizen's Local Reuse Committee (LRC) that would be responsible for the development of a plan to use the facility if and when Warren owned it. In April 1996, the mayor of Warren appointed members to the LRC. A representative from MCC was named to the committee and eventually co-chaired it. The mayor specifically wanted the college involved because of its economic development expertise and the ability of the institution to serve as a broker between the various political factions within the city and within the community. The college was a tremendous asset in the planning process, mainly because of its "social capital"—its reputation within the community to represent broad interests as opposed to specific self-interests.

The LRC met monthly at the college. It held public hearings and hired a consulting firm to develop the plan. From the beginning, the plan articulated a vision for the property that would contain many high-wage, high-skill jobs. The LRC rejected using the facility as a warehouse, which had been proposed by some firms, as well as the creation of an entertainment complex. Neither was deemed to be in the best interest of the community. In addition, the consultant's plan as adopted by the city council called for the establishment of a training center that would be run by the college for those manufacturing firms that might relocate to that site. In this process, MCC played two significant roles: First, because the college was perceived as being neutral ground, it was able to mute the normal contentiousness of local politics and the distrust of many of the principal players. The institution's perspective served to limit and focus the debate and ensure that the ultimate solution would be in the best interests of the community. In that regard, the college was exercising its mission as a proactive player in the area of community development. Second, the college was successful in pointing out that training and education should be part of any new investment in the property.

The plan adopted by the Warren city council called for request for proposals from firms interested in the development of an onsite, college-run training center. The city council hoped to attract high-performance firms that believe that economic development requires the rapid expansion of high-performance manufacturing. This strategy was successful. On the basis of the LRC's plan, the city opened bids for use of the facility. Nine bids were submitted, and four specifically mentioned the establishment of a training center with the college. One of the firms requested that the college write a letter in support of its application, which the firm submitted as part of its proposal to the Warren city council. The winning proposal was from a major builder of welding equipment and body shop systems: DCT Inc. The firm's proposal called for an MCC training center within its new corporate complex. When DCT occupied a portion of the facility in January 1998, the college entered a third stage in its relationship with the property.

STAGE THREE: COLLEGE AS SYSTEMS INTEGRATOR

The final stage required that the college develop a new perspective on economic and workforce development. Like many other community colleges, MCC has been involved in extensive customized training activities with local firms. Although the goal of the college had always been to meet the needs of local companies, the college increasingly believed that it should achieve long-term partnership with companies that would allow the college to meet the human resource needs of local businesses. The college not only would provide on-site worker training but also would assist in the hiring and assessment of new workers. It would become involved in executive training and the design and implementation of company training and policies. In brief, the niche for the college with many manufacturing firms was to be as a human resources "systems integrator."

This long-term perspective also helped the college become a more effective institution. For years, enrollment in the regular instructional occupational programs had declined and graduates became fewer and fewer. The college believed that it was not sufficiently connected with the needs of industry to actually place new students into the workplace. In the last 2 years, the college has begun experimenting with other forms of occupational programs including credit and noncredit programs, modularized curriculum, and "rolling starts," a program that initiates courses at the time of demand, not on the normal semester calendar. Recently, the college took over the Machinist Training Center, originally developed and maintained by the local Work Force Development Board. Its original role of training and placing displaced workers was expanded to train high school students for entry-level machining occupations. The center was located in an industrial park near the campus, simulating a real work experience. The successful experience with this center promoted the concept of locating other "technical centers" within the workplaces of other firms. DCT was a logical choice as a partner in workforce training. MCC had a long history with this firm. The college trained DCT apprentices, and the college was applying for a state economic development and job-training grant to train DCT workers. DCT had also expressed interest in hiring workers from the Machinist Training Center, as well as using college facilities for meetings. At the same time, DCT decided to hire outside providers or use its own personnel to do some additional training and education.

Negotiations with DCT have led to the construction of a new type of corporate center. Although not all the issues have been worked out, the broad outlines of the concept are clear: The new center will be housed within the space currently leased by the company, but it will be maintained and controlled by the college. The company will use college personnel to conduct some of its training, while continuing its relationships with other vendors. The college will have independent access to the site and will be able to use it for the training of other workers, perhaps employees of DCT competitors. In this relationship, both DCT and the college gain. The company has a training partner on site to deliver services to employees. The college gains a site directly within a major company to give a real-world experience to students who want to enter the world of manufacturing. The specific shape of the center and its organization began to become more clear as the company started assuming control of the complex in January 1998.

CONCLUSION

In reviewing the three stages in the partnership between DCT and MCC, we discovered that community colleges must be flexible in their educational delivery systems. We also found just how important community colleges are to the economic development of communities. In all three stages, although the specific activities of the college were different, the overall goal remained the same: the maintenance of high-wage, high-skill jobs in the community. This goal fit not only the economic development mission of the college but also the mission of the community.

Community colleges more and more find that their function is not merely to react to the needs of their communities but to work jointly with community leaders and businesses to shape economic development. This mission can be accomplished in a variety of ways: transfer of technology, modernization of companies, employee assessment and recruitment, and so on. Community colleges must, above all, construct appropriate networks to carry out necessary tasks within their communities. Unlike other postsecondary institutions, the community college is typically a unique product of community involvement and is therefore more likely than most colleges to work with local economic development interests.

Finally, although community colleges work with all types of private-sector businesses, those most likely to benefit from community colleges are small- and medium-sized manufacturing firms. These types of companies make up the fastest growing part of American manufacturing, and they often lack the resources and expertise to deal with modernization and economic development. Community colleges can play an important role in changing the economic fortunes of these firms and their workers. The colleges can become more than trainers and facilitators. They can become economic development leaders, working in conjunction with elected public officials, planners, and the private sector to determine those options that are best for their communities.

Note. From "From Swords to Suppliers: the Role of a Community College in Defense Conversion," by J. Jacobs, 1998, *Economic Development Review, 15*(4), pp. 26–29. Copyright 1998 by American Economic Development Council. Adapted with permission.

World-Class Training Center Helps South Carolina Companies Compete Globally

Don C. Garrison

How should community colleges help economic development efforts in the United States at a time when global competition is growing more fierce? The answer to that question may be found in this case study.

All across America, key players in economic development are keenly aware of the critical role of community and technical colleges in attracting new jobs to their respective communities. Unfortunately, some communities are unaware of the importance of their community colleges; it is the responsibility of community or technical college leaders to publicize the potential contributions of these colleges to economic growth and development. Nationally, the American Association of Community Colleges, representing more than 1,200 institutions, has invested considerable resources to make people aware of the economic development mission of community and technical colleges.

In South Carolina, as well as in neighboring North Carolina, the 2-year college system's birthright lies in economic development. Both states are well known throughout North America and around the world for their ability to attract economic development. In addition, states such as Wisconsin, Delaware, Arizona, and Mississippi view their community and technical colleges as valuable players in economic development. These and other states have involved technical and community colleges in their formula for economic progress.

ECONOMIC DEVELOPMENT IN SOUTH CAROLINA

In 1960, four decades ago, conditions in South Carolina demanded action to stimulate the economy. Young people were leaving the state by the thousands in search of jobs, because job opportunities with promising futures simply were not available here. In fact, the per-capita income in the state ranked at the bottom compared with that of the other states. Today, the trends of outmigration and declining per-capita income have been reversed. Since 1960, the community and technical colleges, county development boards, and the South Carolina Department of Commerce have forged strong partnerships aimed at bringing manufacturing investments to the state.

Here are a few basic statistics that emphasize why manufacturing has been the correct economic development strategy for South Carolina:

- On average over the past 5 years, 24% of the state's workforce has been employed in manufacturing. By comparison, the U.S. average is 16%.
- The average payment per corporate tax return for 1995–1996 was $16,305, nearly 10 times that of the service sector and five times greater than finance, insurance, and real estate companies.
- Manufacturing employees are among South Carolina's best paid, with annual wages that are higher than those in construction, business services, and the retail sector.

In 1996, South Carolina's second consecutive $5-billion-plus investment year was powered by an historic manufacturing performance. Announcements from manufacturers totaled approximately $5.1 billion (or 89% of all activity), continuing a trend that has grown significantly as South Carolina has earned a reputation for business excellence worldwide.

TRI-COUNTY TECHNICAL COLLEGE

These statistics, however, tell only part of the story. For every 100 new manufacturing jobs created in the three counties served by Tri-County Technical College in Pendleton, South Carolina, 64 jobs were created in other sectors. These 64 additional jobs included 45 in wholesale and retail trade, entertainment, and recreation; 7 in transportation; 3 in finance, insurance, and real estate; 3 in business repairs and services; 3 in construction; and 3 in public administration. Statistics show how Tri-County Technical College helps attract manufacturing jobs. In 1997, the South Carolina Tech System's much-heralded Special Schools programs graduated almost 10,000 trainees for the third consecutive year. Approximately half of the graduates trained for new jobs created by industries that expanded their existing operations in South Carolina.

Quite a number of these existing industries reside here in the community, consisting of the three northwestern counties in the state. The I-85 Boom Belt, as it has become known locally and nationally in recent years, stretches through the middle of Tri-County Technical College's district. In recent years, the I-85 Boom Belt has been the focus of national news media.

JACOBS CHUCK MANUFACTURING COMPANY

One of the early investors to the community was Jacobs Chuck Manufacturing Company, whose history parallels that of Tri-County Technical College and the Tech System. (A chuck is a device for holding a drill bit.) Jacobs Chuck Manufacturing was the first company to benefit from the Special Schools training. Its world headquarters is now located here in Clemson, and it continues to flourish, with plants in China, Japan, and Europe. Tri-County Technical College enjoys a powerful partnership with Jacobs, a partnership that has grown as the company has risen to be the world's premier supplier of chucks. Jacobs is where it is today because of strong, effective leadership by a president who embarked on a plan almost 10 years ago to make the company a global competitor.

Although Tri-County Technical College provided training for Jacobs's employees, the college has benefited, in return, from the company's journey to excellence. In 1990, leaders at the college participated in a week-long planning and strategy event conducted for Jacobs by outside consultants. As a result, the college developed a proposal for providing training to Jacobs and other companies. This proposal embraced just-in-time, ISO standards, and other state-of-the-art concepts that have helped participants sustain competitive positions in the global marketplace.

THE WORLD-CLASS TRAINING CENTER

Jacobs's officials, along with representatives of several other manufacturers in the community, reviewed the proposal and gave us a full-speed-ahead directive to launch what is known today as the World-Class Training Center. Since its inception in 1990, the Center has grown to be one of the most outstanding cooperative arrangements in South Carolina. In recent years, the partnership developed initially between Tri-County Technical College and Jacobs has expanded to include several other organizations; the current partnership has 14 corporate members. In addition, the board of directors of the World-Class Training Center extended associate membership to seven local public school districts as well as to the small business members of the local chamber of commerce. The partnership also established formal relationships with several professional organizations, including the American Production and Inventory Control Society, American Society for Quality Control, Society for Human Resource Management, and the Upstate International Trade Association.

In return for membership fees, partnership members receive discounts on training services, exclusive use of an extensive collection of training resources and materials, a seat on the board of directors, direct input into curriculum development, and numerous networking opportunities. Membership fees allow Tri-County Technical College to procure training resources, train and certify instructors, and broker into topical expertise not locally available.

FURTHER BENEFITS

In addition to these direct benefits, the creation of the World-Class Training Center of Tri-County Technical College has led to other advances for members and the community:

- Expansion of the college's service to local industries.
- Addition of world-class topics to the State Tech System's preemployment training curriculum.
- Adoption of total quality management precepts by the college and the public school districts.
- Promotion of tours to world-class facilities throughout the southeast.

Members of the center take an introductory course, the Overview of World-Class Manufacturing, which emphasizes the transformations that are taking place in quality, production, maintenance, and the workforce. The principles studied include total quality management, just-in-time production, total productive maintenance, and teamwork. The source material comes from world leaders such as W. Edwards Deming, Richard Shonberger, Kenneth A. Wantuck, and Peter R. Scholtes.

After this introductory course, members take other courses, including activity-based costing, benchmarking, design of experiment, and failure mode effect analysis, frontline leadership, ISO 9000, self-directed work teams, and statistical process control. Currently, the most popular subjects deal with ISO 9000 and work teams. The members are continually adding new topics for study, and they have formed subgroups to share lessons learned and to provide networking opportunities.

MEMBER COMMENTS

Comments from member companies indicate that the World-Class Training Center is on target with its programs and services:

- "Through the in-house training, field trips, and networking, Ross Operating Valve Company has been able to move forward to become more competitive." —Larry Karnes, plant manager

- "The services Tri-County has provided to Schlumberger have allowed our company to be on the leading edge of world-class manufacturing."—Robin Guyatt, plant manager
- "I think the World-Class Training Center has been a great asset to our company and also to the business community in the Upstate."—Charles Skelton, vice president, Mayfair Mills
- "I look forward to our continued participation in the World-Class Training Center as we further develop the partnership between business, industry, and education to benefit all citizens of our area."—Charles Dalton, president, Blue Ridge Electric Cooperative

Note. From "World-Class Training Center Helps South Carolina Companies Compete Globally," by D. Garrison, 1998, *Economic Development Review, 15*(4), pp. 40–42. Copyright 1998 by American Economic Development Council. Adapted with permission.

CASE 28

Community College of Southern Nevada Looks to Spur Economic Growth

Valerie Miller

Community colleges can do more than just meet employer needs. Indeed, they can spur local economic growth. This case study describes one community college's ambitious efforts to do that.

The Community College of Southern Nevada (CCSN) in Las Vegas wants to be used; that is certainly what its new president would like to see happen. Hoping for the institution to claim its rightful spot in economic development efforts in southern Nevada, CCSN President Richard Carpenter is implementing a new program to reach out to the business community. CCSN's business-training program—the Division of Workforce and Economic Development—is set to be rolled out, and Carpenter admitted that the St. Patrick's Day breakfast meeting will be something of a coming-out party for the program.

"The timing of the NDA is just perfect in that we are launching this," he said. "We are not replacing anything. It is a totally new program." The approximately $200,000 in seed funding for the Division of Workforce and Economic Development endeavor was made possible by what Carpenter called the "streamlining" of some existing programs at the institution, including the demise of most of the official Department of Continuing Education. "It was losing money," said the president. Part of that program was salvaged and incorporated into one of the departments under the Division of Workforce and Economic Development. That department is called Community and Personal Enrichment.

The new division must meet its goal of paying for itself or face being cut or revamped, promised Carpenter. "This has to be 100% self-supporting in a year," he insisted. Failure to do so will not necessarily mean the demise of the division, but it could mean the death of some departments. "A year from now, we may look at four [division departments] that are self-supporting and three that are not, then we will eliminate those three, and it will evolve along that way." Carpenter predicted the program will work with approximately 40 businesses in its first year of operation and move up to approximately 100 clients annually after that.

Other departments to provide business training under the Division of Workforce include the preexisting Adult Literacy Language program, as well as eight other new departments. Those include Transportation, Manufacturing, and Construction; Education and Government; Business Assessment and Consulting; Hospitality; Apprenticeship and Prisons; Health Care and Emergency Services; Retail Services, Banking, and Finance; and CTC/Occupational Safety. More programs could be added if needed, noted Carpenter.

Each department of the division will have its own "workforce specialist" to lead it, and a search will be conducted for the permanent director's spot for the Division of Workforce and Economic Development. Fifteen full-time employees will be working in the division, but it will contract out, as needed, both locally and nationally for consultants and trainers. Debra Solt is now the interim director of the division. She said that although the college had offered workforce training in the past, it was far less extensive and not user friendly. "The old program was confusing to the public," contended Solt. "This is going to be the first call." Among the problems with past business services provided by CCSN, there was a program called "Extended Services," and another one called the "Hospitality Institute," although the Extended Services department also provided hospitality training. "We streamlined all that," explained Solt, "and we're not done streamlining yet."

Even if the old program was difficult to navigate, Somer Hollingsworth, NDA president and chief executive officer, said it still got rave reviews from the business community. "For years, the training that was coming out of the Community College [of Southern Nevada] was excellent," said the NDA chief, who gauged CCSN's performance on surveys filled out by businesses evaluating the training they received. Now, the expectations for the college's program are only higher, he added, although praising Carpenter. "Now, he's going to take it to a totally new level," said Hollingsworth. "We're excited about it." As an incentive to businesses that qualify, the NDA (through state dollars) supplies up to $1,000 per employee for training. That money is normally paid for CCSN training programs when they are available, he explains.

Responding to recent comments made by Senator John Ensign (R-NV) that Nevada's lack of computer science graduates has hurt its technology recruiting efforts, Hollingsworth said although he has not heard that himself, the CCSN training program would help create a technically skilled workforce in the valley. "We've found that what we don't have, we have been able to recruit from out of state," he responded. "You won't always have everything. On the other hand, the community college will help develop a training program."

CCSN's president wants to make sure that his school will become the very first thing economic development leaders like Hollingsworth think of when they pitch the Silver State to businesses. "The March 17 NDA event, I see it as a very opportune time. We hope to really engage in networking," he said. "The most successful marketing tool is when the college is on the front end." CCSN is desperately in need of some marketing, Carpenter added, pointing to the fact that many in the business community are not aware the institution has been doing Microsoft certification for a number of years now. "We need exposure," he lamented. "We need a marketing plan." Hollingsworth agreed that awareness of what programs CCSN offers to the business community is sorely lacking. "No, no," the NDA chief responded when asked if the college's is as recognized as it should be. "It's not his [Carpenter] fault, but I think it hasn't been marketed enough."

Note. From "College Looks to Spur Economic Growth," by V. Miller, 2005, *Las Vegas Business Press, 22*(10), p. 1. Copyright 2005 by *Las Vegas Business Press.* Adapted with permission.

AFTERWORD: LESSONS LEARNED

I n this section, several respected experts—Patrick Gerity, Mark Mervos, Michael Taggart, and Larry Warford—answer a series of questions about the cases in this book and what they believe the role of community colleges is in delivering training; offering business consulting services; and supporting career, community, and economic development. The questions and answers are as follows.

QUESTION 1: AFTER REVIEWING THE CASES IN THIS BOOK, WHAT CONCLUSIONS AND INSIGHTS DO YOU DRAW FROM WHAT WAS PRESENTED?

Gerity: Community colleges in America play a major role in developing people's skills and education, helping employers, supporting communities in good times and bad, and strengthening America's economy. These cases provide evidence that community colleges respond to a variety of community needs and successfully implement positive change and improvement in their communities.

Mervos: Community colleges across the United States are asked to be responsive and flexible to a variety of challenges. Community colleges meet these challenges with limited or no resources and fulfill their mission.

Taggart: The message is clear. Community colleges are critically valuable community partners making sure their communities continually improve as places to live, work, and grow a business. The cases presented in this book illustrate well how proactive colleges do this by designing and delivering programs and services that are making a difference for individuals, families, employers, and communities.

Warford: Community colleges are indeed providing great leadership and collaboration skills in meeting the needs of their communities. The community college can play a variety of roles, and while it often plays a convener role, it can also play other roles.

Question 2: After reviewing the cases in this book, what issues do you believe were left out that should have been covered? What is your own opinion on those issues?

Gerity: This book did not have enough case studies that focused on the development of the minority workforce and the critical role minorities are playing in the current and future growth of the American economy. One other area missed is the current workforce development challenge of retaining and retraining our senior workforce; many business and locations across America do not have young skilled replacement workers available.

Mervos: The issue of credibility of community colleges to assist the various constituents remains a hurdle for the community colleges to address and overcome. Too often the phrase "I didn't know community colleges do that" is heard when community colleges achieve the objective to be accomplished by their community.

Taggart: A worthy focus of a future publication might be how community colleges are partnering with employers of all kinds to improve hiring and promotion success. Many community colleges are successfully targeting the high cost of hiring and promotion decisions that don't work out. Using proven job profiling and worker assessment tools, they are partnering with companies to better design and describe jobs; identify necessary skill requirements; and recruit, employ, train, and promote the best talent. This is an important issue since every day that passes without high-performing people on the job undermines business productivity and innovation.

Warford: I don't necessarily see any issues left out. It is gratifying to see so many and varying partnerships developing.

Question 3: What do you see as the role of the community colleges in training?

Gerity: The community college's role in training is to be recognized as both a community and corporate resource that is prepared to train new workers, train incumbent workers, and train dislocated workers for new jobs. A very important element of community college training is its ability to respond rapidly and effectively. In achieving this, community colleges will be recognized as leaders in workforce development.

Mervos: The role of the community college in training is to provide a competitively skilled workforce that has technical knowledge and is highly productive.

Taggart: Community colleges have many roles related to training. They have an impressive record as community partners and innovators in the planning, development, and delivery of training that contributes to the success of individuals, employers, and communities. They serve as a performance improvement resource for organizations wanting to implement training that has the greatest impact on their business objectives. At the heart of their success is their ability to ground their work in a collaborative dialogue with employers that produces a shared understanding about the gap between the current situation and "the end in mind." On a daily basis they work with employers and organizations of all kinds to produce individual, organizational, and community results from well-executed assessment and training strategies.

Warford: This is what we do, and we should be brought in as partners in all forms of local training. If we don't do training well, we are not doing our job well. I think it is a reasonable goal to have community colleges seen as the "provider of choice" in training situations.

QUESTION 4: WHAT DO YOU SEE AS THE ROLE OF COMMUNITY COLLEGES IN BUSINESS CONSULTING?

Gerity: The community college's role in business consulting is to provide the best customized training and education solutions possible that will solve a company's training or education needs. Experienced community college workforce developers will be able to share with their clients what training has and has not worked in similar situations. It is my recommendation that community college workforce developers pursue training and certification in the following areas: workplace learning and performance, performance consulting, and return-on-investment in training.

Mervos: Community colleges are best suited to provide simple, clear, and relevant solutions for new and seasoned entrepreneurs.

Taggart: Community colleges will continue to be recognized as a valuable source of human resource and business development assistance to current and prospective small business owners. Experienced at partnering, community colleges offer assistance in the form of information and guidance, assessment and training, and performance improvement consulting. They have proven to be savvy in identifying internal and external factors that influence performance and partnering with management to identify performance gaps and the actions required to close those gaps. Colleges help remove impediments to business growth and success.

Warford: I am a bit cautious here. I don't see the strength here. I think we should collaborate with business consultants...not displace or compete with them.

QUESTION 5: WHAT DO YOU SEE AS THE ROLE OF COMMUNITY COLLEGES IN HELPING INDIVIDUALS FORMULATE AND REALIZE THEIR CAREER GOALS?

Gerity: The community college has a core competency of assisting adult learners to formulate and pursue their career goals. Community college faculty have years of experience working with adult learners who want to improve their knowledge and skills to enhance their careers or change their careers. Community colleges have also attracted thousands of college graduates who are in the workplace who enroll part time to learn new software packages or specific technical or business skills. Community colleges specialize in helping adult learners successfully achieve career transitions and building new careers.

Mervos: The community college is in the best position to help individuals develop skills to aid them in formulating and realizing career goals. Community colleges, through partnerships with employers, help individuals find jobs. Furthermore, when community colleges teach individuals about job search strategies, resume writing, and interview skills, they help those individuals to be employed for a lifetime.

Taggart: For many citizens, community colleges have become an easily accessible career navigation resource as they travel an increasingly uncertain career path. Workers find themselves stuck in low-wage jobs or facing the possibility of layoffs. They are confronted with the reality that they must be the managers of their own careers. For many, the local community college has become a resource for answering urgent questions such as what job opportunities best match my interests and aptitudes, or do I have the skills needed for the job or career I want to pursue? Community colleges help individuals develop the skills and confidence they need to plan and manage their own career transitions.

Warford: This is an important goal and should often be done in collaboration with the One Stop center and other WIS staff as well as other agencies and organizations.

QUESTION 6: WHAT DO YOU SEE AS THE ROLE OF COMMUNITY COLLEGES IN SUPPORTING COMMUNITY DEVELOPMENT?

Gerity: Every community college is involved in community development through faculty, administration, and staff participation in and support of community agencies and programs. The community college programming reaches out to citizens in our community ranging from "rocking horse to rocking chair" years to assist with their education, training, and retraining needs. Community colleges receive local, state, and federal funding for their communities. All community colleges play a very active role in their local communities through their board of trustees, administration, faculty, and staff. These key players belong to and serve on boards of many community agencies. Each and every community college has special community-focused programs to support special needs in their communities. We are America's community college.

Mervos: Community colleges should be active partners in community development. Their mission has been and will be to be an integral part of the community by providing both physical and economic access to education and training to the community and its workforce.

Taggart: Community colleges play many roles in supporting community development. They partner with a range of organizations to implement projects important to the futures of their communities. Community colleges serve often as conveners of community stakeholders and are seen as providing a neutral place for them to engage in dialogue and planning. They also share in the leadership for a wide range of projects important to the future of their communities. In our knowledge-based economy, they act upon their shared understanding that communities have better prospects for success when increasing numbers of citizens are improving their knowledge and skills, when the business climate supports innovation and competitiveness, and when the community becomes an even greater place to live, work, and raise a family. Community colleges must continually engage their communities.

Warford: Here again, it is an important role but must be done in collaboration with other community agencies, business, labor, and other organizations.

Question 7: What do you see as the role of community colleges in supporting economic development?

Gerity: Community colleges are very much involved in economic development through their contribution of graduates who are job ready for positions in manufacturing, health care, information technology, biotechnology, and business. Community colleges work closely with economic development agencies in attracting new companies to their region and training students and workers for these new jobs. Community colleges are major players in their local and regional economic development.

Mervos: It is very difficult to find a community college that doesn't support economic development in the geographic area they are located. Their students, their employees, their facilities, and their programs help to attract and support economic development in various forms.

Taggart: A ready supply of workers with up-to-date skills continues to be a key to business attraction and retention and economic development. Community colleges are proven partners in designing and implementing productive economic development strategies. They are an early source of information about the challenges their employer-customers face that often determine whether or not they remain in a community. They are valuable sources of information about the availability to employer-customers of state-sponsored training grants. Increasingly, community colleges are a critical resource for employers' hiring successes as they provide job and skill assessment services that better define required job skills and help identify job applicants who have them. As a training and development resource, colleges enable companies and their workers to continually upgrade key skill sets.

Warford: Very important. At Lane Community College, a few years ago we stepped up our efforts to help recruit "new family-wage jobs" to the area and found that the training function and capability is high on the new and expanding business and industry list. Having an active, competent community college rep at the economic development table is welcomed.

QUESTION 8: WHAT ROLES DO YOU BELIEVE THAT COMMUNITY COLLEGES WILL BE ASKED TO PLAY IN THE FUTURE THAT THEY SO FAR MAY NOT HAVE PLAYED?

Gerity: Community colleges will continue to grow in their role as leaders in workforce, community, and economic development. One critical area for improvement is the community college's ability to respond quickly and effectively in real time to meet the demands of our businesses, communities, and economic development agencies. When community colleges perfect their response time or "speed to market," according to one of our college trustees, then the concept of being a leader in emerging workforce opportunities can become a long-term, sustainable competitive edge for community colleges. The future professional development of community college workforce developers will be an imperative for community colleges to keep pace with rapid rate of change. I believe that this need will be met by the creation of a "National Workforce Development Academy for Community Colleges" that will provide entry-level to advanced training. Community college workforce developers will then be able to develop basic and advanced competencies in workforce development.

Mervos: Because of economic pressures affecting 4-year institutions, community colleges will once again be the most economical access for many to achieve a higher education.

Taggart: Many job seekers and employees not currently served by community colleges might become students if their needs for career management support were met through access to user-friendly places on a college's Web site established for that purpose. Providing easy access to information needed by citizens faced with job changes and uncertainty meets an important community need and might also help the campus successfully address the larger organizational questions such as "How shall we sustain growth in the knowledge economy?" and "How can we maintain or increase community and state support?"

Warford: I think we have pretty well been inducted into the training roles. I believe it's a matter of honing our collaborative skills and those of others.

APPENDIX:
ONLINE RESOURCES

The following are descriptions of selected organizations that provide information and assistance for community colleges interested in training, individual career planning, community development, and economic development.

AMERICAN ASSOCIATION OF COMMUNITY COLLEGES (AACC)
www.aacc.nche.edu
AACC is the primary advocacy organization for the nation's community colleges, a key collaborator with the workforce development community. It serves as a national information resource, creates opportunities for peer networking at all levels, and facilitates collaboration among stakeholders.

AMERICAN SOCIETY FOR TRAINING AND DEVELOPMENT (ASTD)
www.astd.org/astd
ASTD is a worldwide leader in improving performance in the workplace. The association responds to cross-cutting needs concerning career development and lifelong learning issues as they relate to business and industry, national and international governments, and individuals.

CENTER FOR WORKFORCE PREPARATION (CWP)
www.uschamber.com/icw/default
An affiliate organization of the U.S. Chamber of Commerce, CWP is the leader in workforce development strategies, assisting state and local chambers to help their members secure the quality workforce needed to compete in the 21st-century economy.

CENTER FOR WORKFORCE SUCCESS (CWS)
www.nam.org/s_nam/index.asp
An affiliate organization of the National Association of Manufacturers, the mission of CSW is to find and promote workforce solutions for manufacturers in

global economy, in order to build the workforce skills and creative contributions that U.S. industry needs today to strengthen its competitive advantage tomorrow.

CORPORATION FOR A SKILLED WORKFORCE
www.skilledwork.org
CSW is a national nonprofit policy organization based in Ann Arbor, Michigan, created to build workforce development strategies and systems that can produce world-class skill levels.

JOBS FOR THE FUTURE (JFF)
www.jff.org
This organization partners with leaders in education, business, government, and communities around the nation to strengthen opportunities for youth to succeed in postsecondary learning and high-skill careers, increase opportunities for low-income individuals to move into family-supporting careers, and meet the growing economic demand for knowledgeable and skilled workers.

JOHN J. HELDRICH CENTER FOR WORKFORCE DEVELOPMENT
www.heldrich.rutgers.edu
The John J. Heldrich Center for Workforce Development is a research and policy organization dedicated to applying the best research to address the core challenges of New Jersey's and the nation's workforce.

LABOR MARKET INFORMATION TRAINING INSTITUTE (LMI)
www.lmi-net.org
The LMI Training Institute is a comprehensive national LMI training program whose mission is to provide training to LMI professionals and users across the United States and to foster communication within the LMI field. The LMI Training Institute's vision is to "provide an infrastructure to advance the art and science of labor market information among all labor market information professionals and the labor market information customer community."

NATIONAL ASSOCIATION OF STATE WORKFORCE AGENCIES (NASWA)
www.naswa.org
NASWA is an organization of state administrators of unemployment insurance, employment and training services, and labor market information programs. Its mission is to strengthen the National Workforce Development Network through information exchange, liaison, and advocacy. NASWA also operates the Center for Employment Security Education and Research (CESER).

National Association of Counties (NACo)
www.naco.org
NACo serves as a research and educational agency for county officials and other appropriate audiences. Twenty-eight associations of professionally related county officials are affiliated with NACo, including the National Workforce Association. NACo's workforce development program facilitates information sharing about best practices among local elected officials and workforce development organizations.

National Association of State Workforce Board Chairs (NASWBC)
www.subnet.nga.org/workforcecouncilchairs
NASWBC supports its members and their staff directors in their efforts to build state leadership capacity, share best practices among states, promote recognition of state achievements, collectively influence development of federal workforce policy, and become strategic change agents for continuous improvement of the workforce development system. NASWBC is staffed by the Employment and Social Services Policy Studies Division of the National Governors' Association's Center for Best Practices.

National Association of Workforce Boards (NAWB)
www.nawb.org
NAWB represents the interests of the nation's Workforce Investment Boards, the public–private partnerships charged with planning and oversight of local implementation of the Workforce Investment Act.

National Association of Workforce Development Professionals (NAWDP)
www.nawdp.org
NAWDP's mission is to be the national voice for the profession and to meet the individual professional development needs of its membership.

National Career Development Association (NCDA)
www.ncda.org
A division of the American Counseling Association, NCDA's mission is to promote the career development of all people over their life spans. NCDA also speaks for professionalism and standards, and it represents its members' interests before Congress.

NATIONAL COUNCIL FOR CONTINUING EDUCATION AND TRAINING (NCCET)
www.nccet.org
NCCET, an AACC affiliate council, is committed to continuous quality improvement and to quality service as a change agent for lifelong learning. NCCET contributes to individual, community, workforce, and economic development by providing quality education and training services.

NATIONAL COUNCIL FOR WORKFORCE EDUCATION (NCWE)
www.ncwe.org
NCWE , an affiliate of AACC, is committed to promoting excellence in occupational education at the postsecondary level. One of its primary goals is to provide a national forum for administrators and educators in career education and economic development to direct the future role of 2-year colleges in work-related education.

NATIONAL EMPLOYMENT COUNSELING ASSOCIATION (NECA)
www.employmentcounseling.org/neca.html
A division of the American Counseling Association, NECA's mission is to help people prepare for, enter, understand, and progress in the world of work through legislative advocacy, establishing standards and guidelines, showcasing best practices, and networking.

OCCUPATIONAL INFORMATION NETWORK ONLINE
http://online.onetcenter.org
The O*NET system serves as the nation's primary source of occupational information, providing comprehensive information on key attributes and characteristics of workers and occupations. The O*NET database houses these data and O*NET OnLine provides easy access to that information.

WORKFORCE ALLIANCE
www.workforcealliance.org
The Alliance is a network of local workforce development experts: employers, training providers, and local officials charged with preparing workers for skilled jobs in cities and states throughout the country.

INDEX

Aa

Aaron-Selph, Roxanne, 120
Academy of Culinary Arts, Atlantic City
   CC's, 52
accountability
   Career Pathways model as tool for, 88
   Elizabethtown Community and
      Technical College health-care
      training challenge and, 88–90
Ad Hoc Task Force on Homeland
   Security, AACC's, 71
Adult Education, Kentucky, 84
Adult Literacy Language program, CC of
   Southern Nevada's, 178
Advanced Manufacturing for the 21st
   Century career pathways model.
   See Owensboro Community and
   Technical College, KY
Airtex Corporation, 18
Aleris, 103
Amatrol, Inc., 103
American Association of Community
   Colleges (AACC)
   Ad Hoc Task Force on Homeland
      Security, 71
   characteristics and contact
      information, 187

Economic Development Award, 159
on economic development mission of
   community and technical
   colleges, 171
homeland security and, 3
on JCCC/BNSF Railroad partnership,
   154
American Counseling Association, 189
American Society for Training and Devel-
   opment (ASTD), 187
Apprenticeship and Prisons Department,
   CC of Southern Nevada's, 178
apprenticeships, information technology,
   73–78
Arizona, community and technical colleges
   and economic development in, 171
Army Corps of Engineers, 124
Artpark, NY, 64
Atlantic Cape Community College,
   Atlantic City, NJ, 2–3, 49–50, 51–54
Atlantic Cape May Workforce Investment
   Board (WIB), 51, 52, 53
Atlantic City Casino Training Consor-
   tium, 51–52
Atlantic City First Job Readiness Program
   (AC First), 49–50, 51–52
auto production, Detroit Tank Arsenal
   and, 164–165
Autry, Gerald, 21, 23

Bb

Baker, Amy, 68, 69
Banking Consortium, northeast Texas, 45–47
Baroody, Tim, 114
Barton, Thomas E., Jr., 42
best practices, EPA Brownfields Job Training Program, 123–124
Binkley, Tim, 108
Blue Ridge Electric Cooperative, SC, 175
Blue Steel Tool, 23
BMW plant, in upstate South Carolina, 41
Borger, Mark, 56
Bridgeport Economic Resource Center, CT, 132
Briggs, Mark, 43
Brown, Deborah, 46
Brown, Michael, 67–68
Brownfields Assessment Pilots, 117–118. *See also* EPA Brownfields Job Training Program
Brownfields Economic Redevelopment, 117
Brownfields Worker Training Grants, 118
Bucks County Community College, Newtown, PA, 3, 73
    Center for Business & Industry Training, 74, 75–76, 77
Buffalo State College, NY, 64
Bureau for Career and Technical Education Apprenticeship Program, PA, 75
Burlington Northern Santa Fe (BNSF) Railroad
    associate degree in railroading and, 153–154
    conclusion, 155
    credit instruction and, 153
    economic benefit to Johnson County and, 153
    funding JCCC cooperative with, 151–152
    impact of JCCC partnership with, 154–155
    instructional design and support for JCCC program, 152–153
    Johnson County CC partnership with, 5
    partnership and plan with JCCC Business and Industry Institute, 150–151
    training headquarters, 149
    Training Systems Development group, 152
Business & Industry Services Network (CT), 121
Business and Industry Services Division, Gateway Community and Technical College, KY, 93
Business Assessment and Consulting Department, CC of Southern Nevada's, 178
business connections, Career Pathways model as tool for, 87
business consulting
    community college, 61
    experts on role of community colleges in, 183
    homeland security programs, 67–71
    Lockheed Martin IS&S IT apprenticeship program, 73–78
    Niagara County CC, Sanborn, NY, 63–65
Business Partnership Development Program, Springfield Technical CC, MA, 127–130
Butler, Johnny, 75
Butt, Ed, 154

Cc

Caesars Atlantic City, NJ, 52
Camden, NJ, Brownfields Assessment Demonstration Pilot program and, 121

Campaign for Growth and Manufacturing Renewal, NAM's, 112
Carberry, Gail, 128, 129, 130
Career and Education Center, Elizabethtown, KY, 84
career development
community colleges and, 79
Elizabethtown Community and Technical College, KY, 82–91
entrepreneurs in Virginia, 113–114
experts on role of community colleges in, 183–184
Gateway Community and Technical College, KY, 93–97
Kentucky Community and Technical College System, 81–82
in manufacturing, 111–112
Owensboro Community and Technical College, KY, 99–105
Winston Salem Brownfields Environmental Job Training Program, 107–109
Carl D. Perkins Vocational and Technical Education Act, 136
Carlsen, Charles J., 150
Carnegie Mellon University's Software Engineering Institute (SEI), 70–71
Carpenter, Richard, 177–178, 179
Casino Reinvestment Development Authority, NJ, 53
Cavagnaro, Charles, 128, 129
Center for Accelerated Technology Training (CATT), 2, 39–43
Center for Business & Industry Training (CBIT), Bucks County CC, Newtown, PA, 74, 75–76, 77
Center for Business and Industry Services, Middlesex CC, Middletown, CT, 121
Center for Community and Economic Development (CCED), Owensboro Community and Technical College, KY, 100

Center for Employment Security Education and Research (CESER), 188
Center for Entrepreneurial Development, Richmond, VA, 4, 113
Center for Workforce Development and Policy at Macomb CC in Warren, MI, 135
Center for Workforce Preparation (CWP), 187
Center for Workforce Success (CWS), 187–188
Century Aluminum, 103
"Certified Workforce," KY, 87
Chapman, Dale, 15, 17
Chrysler Corporation, 165
Cincinnati Primary Metropolitan Statistical Area, 93
Clean Harbors (MA remediation company), 122
Clearwater Systems EEC, 120
Clements Group, 128, 129
Clevenger, Charles, 56
ClientLogic service center, Williamsburg County, SC, 42, 43
Clinton, Hillary, 70
Coalition for a Better Acre, Lowell, MA, 121
Coffman Foundation, 114
College Center of the Finger Lakes, Corning, NY, 11, 13–14
Collegis Corporation, 18
Colorado Community Colleges and Occupational Education System (CCCOES)
accelerated career academies, 160–161
conclusion, 162
economic development and community college education under, 158–159
economic development as primary goal of, 5, 158

economic development successes of, 159–160

formation of, 157–158

Workplace Learning Project, 161–162

Colorado FIRST (For Inspiration and Recognition of Science and Technology), 160

Colorado Governor's Job Training Office, 159

Colorado Governor's Office of Business Development, 159

Colorado Literacy Programs, 162

Colorado Small Business Administration, 159

Colorado State Board for Community Colleges and Occupational Education, 157, 159

Colorado's Existing Industry Customized Training Programs, 160

Commonwealth of Pennsylvania, 57

Commonwealth of Pennsylvania Office of Science Technology and Workforce, 142

Community and Personal Enrichment, CC of Southern Nevada's, 177–178

Community College of Allegheny County (CCAC), Pittsburgh, PA, 70–71

Community College of Denver Technical Education Centers, 161

Community College of Rhode Island, 122

Community College of Southern Nevada (CCSN), Las Vegas, 5, 177–179

Community College Workforce Alliance, Richmond, VA, 4, 113, 114

community development

Brownfields sites' revitalization and, 117–125

community college career and technical education programs and, 135–136

community colleges and, 115

employers' needs for entry-level talent, 131–133

experts on role of community colleges in, 184–185

predicting industry's future needs, 127–130

community strategic partnerships, Career Pathways model as tool for, 87

COMPASS testing centers, 83

CompXNational, Mauldin, SC, 42

Congressional Budget Office, 164

Connecticut Department of Labor, 120

Cooperative Education Program, Housatonic CC, Bridgeport, CT, 131–133

Corning, Inc., 11

Corporation for a Skilled Workforce, 188

Council for Adult and Experiential Learning, 6

Council for Economic Development, 125

Council for Urban Economic Development, 119

CTC/Occupational Safety Department, CC of Southern Nevada's, 178

Cultural Education Center, Johnson County CC, Overland Park, KS, 153

Cunningham, Ray, 21

Dd

DANA Corporation, 103

Danville Community College, VA, 22

Davis, Edward, 109

Davis, Jim, 23

DCT Inc., Detroit Tank Arsenal closing and, 167, 168

Delaware, community and technical colleges and economic development in, 171

Delta College, Midland, MI, 11–12, 14

Detroit Tank Arsenal

downsizing at, 163

Local Reuse Committee's plans for, 166–167
Macomb CC retraining for, 5, 165–166
Macomb County and, 164–165
Dillard, Ben, 41–42
Discover College, Owensboro Community and Technical College, KY, 99
Division of Workforce and Economic Development, CC of Southern Nevada's, 177–179
Dorcas Place, RI, 122
Doubletree Hotel, Overland Park, KS, 153
Dow Chemical, 11–12, 14
Driving Change in Community Colleges, Ford Foundations report on, 124
DuBois Educational Foundation Workforce Development and Technology Center at Pennsylvania State University-DuBois, 146
Dyersburg State Community College, TN, 2, 21–23
Dynamic Technology Systems, 34, 37

Ee

Eastern Niagara Chamber of Commerce, NY, 65
Eavenson, Harold, 46
economic development
Career Pathways model as tool for, 86–87
Colorado community colleges and, 157–162
community college as training center, 149–155
community colleges and, 137
Elizabethtown Community and Technical College health-care training challenge and, 88–90
experts on role of community colleges in, 185

JCCC–BNSF partnership and, 149–155
lean manufacturing training, 139–147
military base conversions and, 163–169
Tri-County Technical College, Pendleton, SC, 172–175
ECS Ltd., Greensboro, NC, 108
Education and Government Department, CC of Southern Nevada's, 178
Education and Training Resource Guide, WEDnetPA's, 57–58
80/20 corporate philosophy, 145
Eisen, Phyllis, 111, 112
Elizabethtown Community and Technical College (KY) Career Pathways
as career system model, 83–84
health-care training challenge, 88–90
nine key principles for, 85–88
origin of, 82–83
partnership for, 84–85
Ellison, Jan, 50
Employment and Social Services Policy Studies Division of the National Governors' Association's Center for Best Practices, 189
Engineering Tectonics PA of Winston-Salem, 108
Ensign, John, 178
Enterprise Ohio Network, 57
Envirofox (hazmat control vehicle), 165–166
Enviromed, 120
Environmental Business Council of New England, 122
environmental justice, EPA Brownfields Job Training Program and, 119
EPA Brownfields Job Training and Development Demonstration Pilot, 121
EPA Brownfields Job Training Program, 4
background of, 117–118
conclusion, 124–125

environmental justice and, 119
in Mid-Connecticut, 119–121
other community-based partnerships
and best practices, 121–124
training opportunities under, 118–119
EPA Brownfields Worker Training Grants,
118, 119–121

Ff

Fairmont State Community and Technical
College (FSC&TC), WV, 68–69
Farmis Inc., NY, 64–65
Federal Emergency Management Agency
(FEMA), 67–68, 69
Federal Hill House, RI, 122
financial aid, for Owensboro Community
and Technical College Career
Pathways program, 104
Fire and Police Training Center for Profes-
sional Development and Homeland
Security, Owens CC, OH, 67–68
Ford, Henry, 141
Ford Bridges to Opportunities State
Team, 84
Ford Foundations, 82, 88, 102, 124
Forsyth County (NC) Environmental
Affairs, 108
Forsyth Technical Community College,
Winston-Salem, NC, 4, 108
Foster, Brantley, 45
Frontier Community College, IL, 18
funding, Career Pathways model as lever
for, 86

Gg

Garrett, Franklin, 43
Gateway Community and Technical
College, KY
Career Pathways initiative, 82, 94–95
challenge for Career Pathways initia-
tive of, 95–96
lessons learned, 96–97
overview of, 93–94
Geelan, Marie, 131
General Dynamics, 164. *See also* Detroit
Tank Arsenal
General Dynamics Land Systems, 165
Genesee State College, NY, 64
Genesis Center, RI, 122
Gentile, Paul, 56
George Mason University's Institute for
Public Policy, 34, 36
Geoscience & Technology PA of Winston-
Salem, 108
Gerity, Patrick
on business consulting role of
community colleges, 183
on career development role of
community colleges, 183–184
on case studies, 182
on community college role in U.S.,
181
on community development role of
community colleges, 184
on economic development role of
community colleges, 185
on future roles of community
colleges, 186
on training role of community
colleges, 182
WEDnetPA and, 56
Gilkison, Don, 13, 15
Gilmore, Davey, 59–60
Ginn, David T., 43
Goldenbaum, Don, 150
Goodyear Maintenance Technician Co-op
Program, 2, 21–23
Goodyear Tire and Rubber Company, 21
Gorko, Richard, 63
Gorkowski, Rosanne, 35
Great Plains Technical School, Lawton,
OK, 21–22

Greater Owensboro Chamber of Commerce, 103
Greater Owensboro Economic Development Corporation, 103
Green River Area Development District, 102
Greenville Technical College, SC, 41–42
Groundwork Providence Brownfields Job Training and Development Program, 122
Groundwork Providence (RI), 118
Guaranteed Free Training (GFT), PA, 3, 55, 56
Guaranty Bank, TX, 45, 47

Hh

Hardin Memorial Hospital, KY, 84
Harrah's Casino Hotel, Atlantic City, NJ, 49, 50
Hascall, Jim, 16
Health Care and Emergency Services Department, CC of Southern Nevada's, 178
health-care industry. *See* career development
Health Professional Institute (HPI), Atlantic City CC's, 53
Heberling, Bob, 140, 145
Heldrich (John J.) Center for Workforce Development, 188
Higher Education Advanced Technology Center at the former Lowry Air Force Base, CO, 161
Higher Learning Commission, 18
Hoffman-LaRoche plant, Florence, SC, 41
Hollings, Ernest F., 40
Hollingsworth, Somer, 178–179
homeland security
    AACC/League for Innovation in the Community College and, 3, 71

Fairmont State Community and Technical College, WV and, 68–69
    Monroe CC, Rochester, NY and, 69–70
    Owens CC, OH program, 67–68
    Software Engineering Institute in Pittsburgh and, 70–71
Homeland Security Initiative, League for Innovation in the Community College's, 71
Homeland Security Management Institute, Monroe CC, Rochester, NY, 69–70
Horrell, Dorothy, 159–160
Hospitality Department, CC of Southern Nevada's, 178
hospitals. *See also* career development
    community colleges' partnerships with, 128, 129–130
    NorthStar Healthcare Initiative, KY and, 83, 90–91
    Technology Retraining Internship Program and, 36
Housatonic Community College (HCC), Bridgeport, CT, 4, 131–133
Hudgins, James L., 39, 40
Hunn, David, 36, 37
Hussain, Fayyaz, 64–65

Ii

I-85 Boom Belt, SC, 173
Illinois Community College Board, 18
Illinois Department of Commerce and Economic Opportunity, 17
Industrial Technical Center, Johnson County CC, Overland Park, KS, 151
Industry Modular Accessible Credentials (IMAC), 102, 103
information technology. *See also* career development

Lockheed Martin Information Systems & Solutions apprenticeship program, 73–78
Information Technology Association of America, 34
Institute for Service Excellence (ISE), Atlantic City, NJ, 53
institutional transformation, Career Pathways model and, 85–86
International City Managers Association, 125
International Institute, RI, 122
International Trade Center Small Business Development Center, Niagara Falls, NY, 63–64
ISO 9000, World-Class Training Center, Tri-County Technical College, Pendleton, SC and, 174

Jj

Jacobs, James, 135, 136
Jacobs Chuck Manufacturing Company, Tri-County Technical College, Pendleton, SC and, 173–174
James, Patricia, 49, 50
Jobs for the Future (JFF), 188
Jobs for Youth (JFY) Networks, Boston, MA, 122
John J. Heldrich Center for Workforce Development, 188
Johnson County Community College (JCCC), Overland Park, KS
associate degree in railroading from, 153–154
BNSF partnership with, 5
BNSF Railroad partnership and plan, 150–151
BNSF Railroad training center at, 149
conclusion, 155
credit instruction, 153
economic benefit to Johnson County, 153
funding the cooperative with BNSF Railroad, 151–152
impact of BNSF Railroad partnership with, 154–155
instructional design and support, 152–153
Johnson County Business and Industry Institute at, 150
local economic development and, 149–150

Kk

Kaizen events and teams, at Triangle Suspension Systems, DuBois, PA, 140
Kaw Area Technical School, Topeka, KS, 22
Keeping America Competitive: How a Talent Shortage Threatens U.S. Manufacturing (2003), 111
Kentucky Cabinet for Health and Family Services, 84
Kentucky Community and Technical College System Career Pathways, 3, 81–91
nine key principles for, 85–88
origins of, 82–83
partnership for, 84–85
Kentucky Community and Technical College System (KCTCS)
Elizabethtown, 82–91
Gateway, 93–97
Owensboro, 99–105
Kentucky Department for Employment Services, 102
Kentucky Department of Labor, 89
Kentucky Employability Certificate, 87, 99, 100
Kentucky Manufacturing Skills Standards, 87
Kentucky Postsecondary Education Im-

provement Act, 82
Kimberly Clark, 103
Kinyon, David, 65
Klock, Michael and Susan, 65
Kravco-Simon Developers, Atlantic City, NJ, 53

Ll

Labor Market Information Training Institute (LMI), 188
Lamm, Richard D., 157
Law and Justice Academic Program, Monroe CC, Rochester, NY, 70
League for Innovation in the Community College
    College and Career Transitions Initiative, 88
    Homeland Security Initiative of, 3, 71
lean manufacturing
    benefits, 144–146
    collaborative planning for Triangle Suspension Systems, 142–143
    description of, 141–142
    summary, 147
    training at Triangle Suspension Systems in, 143–144
    at Triangle Suspension Systems, DuBois, PA, 140
Lewis and Clark Community College, Godfrey, IL
    building a partnership, 11–13
    Center for Workforce Training, 17
    defining the problem, 13–14
    lessons learned, 18–19
    Olin Corporation and, 2, 11–19
    PC Institute at, 16
    problem analysis, 14–17, 15t
    results and benefits, 17–18
Linking Training to Performance: A Guide for Workforce Development Professionals, 1, 6

Little, Geoff, 127–128, 129
Local Reuse Committee (LRC), Detroit Tank Arsenal and, 166–167
Lockheed Martin Information Systems & Solutions (IS&S), King of Prussia, PA, IT apprenticeship program, 3, 73–78
Lumina Foundation, Achieving the Dream initiative, 88

Mm

Maas, Brian, 108
Machinist Training Center, Macomb CC, Warren, MI, 168
Macomb Community College (MCC), Warren, MI
    characteristics, 165
    DCT partnership with, 168–169
    economic development and, 5, 163
    as planner in base closing and reuse, 166–167
    retraining Detroit Tank Arsenal workers, 165–166
    as systems integrator upon Detroit Tank Arsenal closing, 167–168
Macomb County, MI, Detroit Tank Arsenal and, 164–165
Mahon, Jack, 56
Maintenance Technician Co-Op Program, Obion County, TN, 23
manufacturers, community colleges' partnerships with, 128, 129
manufacturing. See also lean manufacturing
    careers in, 111–112
    in SC, Tri-County Technical College and, 172–173
Marin Environmental, 120
Marmon Group, The, 145
Marmon Highway Technologies, 146
Marshall, Roy, 35
Martinez, Rita, 112

Mayfair Mills, SC, 175
McCormick, James, 59–60
McCormick, Rich, 69
McCullough, Sam, 60
McKnight, Regina, 41
mentors, for Lockheed Martin IS&S IT
    apprenticeship program, 77
Meriden (CT) National Association for
    the Advancement of Colored People
    (NAACP), 120
Mervos, Mark
    on business consulting role of
        community colleges, 183
    on career development role of
        community colleges, 184
    on case studies, 182
    on community college role in U.S.,
        181
    on community development role of
        community colleges, 184
    on economic development role of
        community colleges, 185
    on future roles of community
        colleges, 186
    on training role of community
        colleges, 182
Metropolitan Community College,
    Omaha, NE, 17–18
Michael, Larry, 56
Middlesex Community College, Middle-
    town, CT, 119–121
Middlesex County Soil and Water Con-
    servation District, CT, 120
Middlesex (CT) National Association for
    the Advancement of Colored People
    (NAACP), 119–120
Midland Center, Dow Chemical, Delta
    College and, 14
military spending, national economy and,
    164
Mirage Resorts, Atlantic City, NJ, 49

Mississippi, community and technical
    colleges and economic development
    in, 171
Monroe Community College (MCC),
    Rochester, NY, Homeland Security
    Management Institute of, 69–70
Myers, Lee, 56, 59–60

Nn

National Academy of Railroad Sciences
    (NARS), 152, 154
National Association of Counties
    (NACo), 189
National Association of Manufacturers
    (NAM), 4, 111–112, 187–188
National Association of State Workforce
    Agencies (NASWA), 188
National Association of State Workforce
    Board Chairs (NASWBC), 189
National Association of Workforce Boards
    (NAWB), 189
National Association of Workforce Devel-
    opment Professionals (NAWDP), 189
National Career Development Association
    (NCDA), 189
National Council for Continuing Educa-
    tion and Training (NCCET), 190
National Council for Workforce Educa-
    tion (NCWE), 190
National Dissemination Center for Career
    and Technical Education at The Ohio
    State University, 135
National Employment Counseling
    Association (NECA), 190
National Environmental Justice Advisory
    Council, 124
National Governors' Association's Center
    for Best Practices, Employment and
    Social Services Policy Studies Divi-
    sion of, 189

National Institute of Standards and Technology (NIST), Manufacturing Extension Partnership, 142, 143–144

National Retail Federation, 53

National Science Foundation (NSF) Advanced Technology Education grants, 136

National Workforce Development Network, 188

National Workplace Literacy Program grants, for Colorado programs, 162

Neal, Stu, 114

New Britain (CT) National Association for the Advancement of Colored People (NAACP), 120

New England Training and Consulting, 120

New Jersey Business and Industry Association (BIA), 26

New Jersey Commerce Commission, 26, 28–29

New Jersey Community College Consortium for Workforce and Economic Development, 2, 25–31

New Jersey Council of County Colleges, 25–26, 28

New Jersey Department of Human Services, 29–30

New Jersey Department of Labor and Workforce Development, 26, 27–29, 51, 53

New Jersey Department of Treasury, 26

New Jersey Health Initiatives, Robert Wood Johnson Foundation's, 53

New Jersey Institute of Technology, 121

New Jersey Youth Corps, 121

New Opportunities of Greater Meriden, CT, 120

New York Department of Labor, 64

Newark, NJ, Brownfields Assessment Demonstration Pilot program and, 121

Newman, Robert, 65

Newton, PA, 3

Niagara County Community College, Sanborn, NY, 3, 63–65

Niagara County Industrial Development Agency (IDA), 64, 65

Niagara Sports Arena, Olcott, NY, 65

Niagara USA Chamber of Commerce, 65

North Carolina, community and technical colleges and economic development in, 171

North End Action Team (CT), 120

Northeast Texas Community College, Mount Pleasant, Skills Development Program, 2, 45–47

Northeast Utilities System, 120

Northern Kentucky Community College, 93

Northern Kentucky Council of Partners in Education K–16, 95

Northern Kentucky One Stop, 95

Northern Kentucky University, 93

Northern Virginia Community College, Annandale, VA, 2
  Technology Retraining Internship Program (TRIP), 33–37

Northern Virginia Regional Partnership Inc. (NVRP), 34–35
  Regional Workforce Development Coordinating Center, 36

NorthStar Healthcare Initiative, KY, 83, 90–91

Northwest Pennsylvania Industrial Resource Center, Erie, PA, 5, 142, 147

Northwest Pennsylvania Industrial Resource Center (NWIRC), Erie, PA, 140

Northwest Piedmont Council of Governments' Workforce Development, The (NC), 108

Oo

Obion County Chamber of Commerce, 23

Obion County Industrial Development Corporation (OCIDC), 21, 22

Occupational Education System, CO, 5

Occupational Information Network On-line (O*NET), 190

Occupational Safety and Health Administration (OSHA), 16, 119

Office of Economic Development, Stafford County, VA, 113

Office of International Research, Johnson County CC, Overland Park, KS, 150

Ohio Board of Regents, 6

Ohio Fire Academy, 68

Ohno, Taichi, 141

Olin Center for Excellence, 14, 16–17

Olin Corporation, Lewis and Clark CC and, 2, 11–19

Olin/Lewis and Clark Education Alliance, 11, 12, 13–15, 19

One-Stop Career Centers
Brownfields Worker Training Grants and, 118–119
Career Pathways, WIBs and, 87
New Jersey WIB as, 53
Northern Kentucky, 94, 95
NorthStar Healthcare Initiative as, 83
Owensboro, KY, 100, 102

open entry or exit, for Owensboro Community and Technical College Career Pathways program, 104

Orr, Cheryl, 34, 37

Overland Park, KS
funding BNSF–Johnson County CC cooperative and, 151–152
industrial revenue bonds for BNSF training center in, 150

Owens Community College (OCC), OH, Fire and Police Training Center for

Professional Development and Homeland Security of, 67–68

Owensboro Community and Technical College, KY
Career Pathways initiative, 82, 100
challenge for Career Pathways initiative, 101
implementation of Career Pathways initiative, 103–104
lessons learned, 104–105
overview of, 99
partners for Career Pathways initiative, 102–103

Owensboro One-Stop, 102

Pp

P–16 Council, KY, 84

Payne, Clifton A., 47

Peddinghaus, in Andrews, SC, 41

Pehote, Harry, 144, 145, 146

Penn State DuBois, 5

Pennsylvania, Guaranteed Free Training (GFT) program in, 3, 55, 56

Pennsylvania College of Technology, 56, 57, 58, 59

Pennsylvania Commission for Community Colleges (PCCC), 55–56

Pennsylvania Department of Community and Economic Development (DCED), 55–56, 58, 59

Pennsylvania Department of Education, 75

Pennsylvania Department of Labor and Industry, 58, 73, 75

Pennsylvania Department of Labor Law and Compliance, 75

Pennsylvania State System of Higher Education (PA State System), 55–56, 57, 59

Pennsylvania State University-DuBois, 140, 142, 146

Pennsylvania State University (PSU), 3, 73, 74, 77
Perkins Act, Career Pathways model and, 88
Perrone, John J., Jr., 69, 70
Philadelphia, School District of, 73, 75
Philadelphia Youth Network (PYN), 73, 75
Pierpoint, Paul, 56
Pikes Peak Community College Commerce Centers, Colorado Springs, CO, 161
Plan for Progress, Springfield, MA, 128
Plows, Nancy, 140
Porten, Hank, 128, 129–130
Postsecondary Education Improvement Act (1997), 93
Price, Jim, 23
Providence Department of Planning and Development, 122
Public Safety Training Center, Monroe CC, Rochester, NY, 69–70
public–private partnership myths, 155
Pueblo Community College Gorsich Advanced Technology Center, CO, 161

Rr

Rail Safety Improvement Act (1988), 154
Red Rocks Community College Business Institute, Lakewood, CO, 161
Reich, Robert, 154
Retail Services, Banking, and Finance Department, CC of Southern Nevada's, 178
Rhode Island Department of Environmental Management, 122
Rhode Island Economic Development Corporation, 122
Riddle, Cathy, 114
Ritchie, James J., 132
Robert C. Byrd National Aerospace Education Center, OH, 69

Robert Wood Johnson Foundation, New Jersey Health Initiatives, 53
Rocky Mountain News, 158
Romer, Roy, 159
Roper, Keisha, 107
Ross Operating Valve Company, SC, 174
Royal Guard Vinyl, 22
Rubenzahl, Ira, 128

Ss

Sakwa, Michele, 108
Salonen, Neil A., 132
School-to-Work program, Macomb CC, Warren, MI, 165
Shell Oil, 16
Shenzhen Polytechnic, Shenzhen Guangdong, China, 18
Shingo, Shigeo, 144
Siegel-Robert (SR) Products, 22–23
Single Minute Exchange of Dies (SMED), 144
SkillTrain Center, Owensboro Community and Technical College, KY, 99, 100, 103
Small Business Development Center, Niagara County CC, Sanborn, NY, 63–65
Small Business Liability Relief and Brownfields Revitalization Act (2002), 117, 118, 119
Soldano, Jack, 64
Solt, Debra, 178
South Carolina
    Center for Accelerated Technology Training, 2, 39–43
    community and technical colleges and economic development in, 171
    economic development in, 172
South Carolina Department of Commerce, 172

South Jersey Hospitality Opportunities for Potential Employees (SJ HOPE), 52

Southern Illinois University at Carbondale, Lewis and Clark CC and, 16

Southern Illinois University School of Engineering, 12

Southwest Illinois Advanced Manufacturing Program, 12

Special Schools programs, South Carolina Tech System's, 172

Spoon River Community College, Canton, IL, 18

Springfield Technical Community College, MA, 4

Springfield Technical Community College (STCC), Springfield, MA, 127–130

Spry, Craig, 109

Stamford, CT, EPA Brownfields Job Training Pilot Program in, 122–123

Stark, Dan, 56

Stop Wasting Abandoned Property, RI, 122

Tt

Taber, Mike, 108–109

Taggart, Michael
on business consulting role of community colleges, 183
on career development role of community colleges, 184
on case studies, 182
on community college role in U.S., 181
on community development role of community colleges, 184–185
on economic development role of community colleges, 185
on future roles of community colleges, 186
on training role of community

colleges, 182–183

WEDnetPA and, 57

Taste of Buffalo (NY), A, 64

Taste of Lewiston (NY), A, 64

Taylor, Steve, 42

Tech Prep program, Macomb CC, Warren, MI, 165

Technology Reinvestment Program (TRP), U.S. DOD's, 165–166

Technology Retraining Internship Program (TRIP), 33–37

Temporary Assistance to Needy Families (TANF), 49–50
Latina, in South Jersey, 52

Tennessee Board of Regents, 23

Tennessee Technology Center, Newbern, TN, 21

Texas Workforce Commission, 45–47

Third Frontier Network (TFN), OH, 68

3RC, 107, 108

Tighe & Bond Inc., 120

Total Productive Maintenance (TPM), 141, 144

Toyota, lean manufacturing by, 141·

training for individuals and employers
Atlantic Cape CC and Atlantic Cape May WIB, 51–54
Atlantic City (NJ) First Job Readiness Program, 49–50
Banking Consortium, northeast Texas, 45–47
Center for Accelerated Technology Training, SC, 39–43
community colleges and, 9
Dyersburg State CC, TN, 21–23
experts on role of community colleges in, 182–183
Lewis and Clark CC, IL, and Olin Corporation, 11–19
New Jersey Community College Consortium for Workforce and Economic Development, 25–31

Technology Retraining Internship Program, VA, 33–37

WEDnetPA, 55–60

transition programs, Career Pathways model as, 86

Transportation, Manufacturing, and Construction Department, CC of Southern Nevada's, 178

Travelers Aid Society, RI, 122

Tri-County Technical College, Pendleton, SC

economic development and, 5, 172–173

Jacobs Chuck Manufacturing Company and, 173–174

World-Class Training Center at, 173–175

Triangle Suspension Systems (TSS), DuBois, PA

background of, 139–140

benefits of lean manufacturing for, 144–146

collaborative effort for lean manufacturing at, 142–143

implementing lean manufacturing at, 143–144

lean manufacturing training effects on, 147

need for change, 140

tuition and tuition refund, for Owensboro Community and Technical College Career Pathways program, 104

Tupperware, in Hemingway, SC, 41

Uu

Unger, Paul, 68

Unilever, 103

Union City, TN, 21, 22

Union City *Messenger*, 22

United Automobile Workers (UAW), 165

United Biochemicals, NY, 64–65

University of Bridgeport, CT, 132–133

University of Findlay, OH, 68

University of South Carolina's Moore School of Business, 41

upward mobility. *See also* career development

Career Pathways model as tool for, 87–88

U.S. Chamber of Commerce, Center for Workforce Preparation and, 187

U.S. Department of Commerce Economic Development Administration, 53

U.S. Department of Commerce's Office of Technology Policy, 34, 36

U.S. Department of Defense (DOD), 165–166

U.S. Department of Education, 82

National Workplace Literacy Program grants of, 162

U.S. Department of Labor, 40, 109

U.S. Environmental Protection Agency (EPA), 107, 117. *See also* EPA Brownfields Job Training Program

U.S. General Accounting office, workforce development study by, 124

U.S. National Guard Bureau, 70

U.S. Small Business Administration, 63

Vv

Vanasse Hangen Brustlin, Inc., 120

Vaughan, George B., 43

Vaughn Electric Company, 22

Villa Fortunata's of Lewiston, NY, 64

Virginia

career development to entrepreneurs in, 113–114

northern, Technology Retraining Internship Program in, 33–37

Voelker, Mike, 150–151

Ww

Walcoff & Associates Inc., 35
Warford, Larry
on business consulting role of
community colleges, 183
on career development role of
community colleges, 184
on case studies, 182
on community college role in U.S.,
181
on community development role of
community colleges, 185
on economic development role of
community colleges, 185
on future roles of community
colleges, 186
on training role of community
colleges, 182–183
Wartgow, Jerome F., 157–158
WEDnetPA Action Team, 56–57, 59
WEDnetPA Executive Committee, 59
WEDnetPA (Workforce and Economic
Development Network of Pennsylvania), 55–60
Weyerhaeuser, 103
White, Pete, 35, 37
WIA. See Workforce Investment Act
Williamsburg County School District,
SC, 40–41
Williamsburg Technical College, SC, 40–
41, 43
Williamson, James C., 41
Wilson, Howard, 142–143
Winston Salem Brownfields Environmen-
tal Job Training Program, 107–109

Wisconsin, community and technical col-
leges and economic development in,
171
Womack, J. P., 141
Woodward, Douglas P., 41
Work Force Development Board, Warren,
MI, 168
"Workforce 2020: Work and Workers in
the 21st Century," 40
Workforce Alliance, 86, 190
Workforce and Economic Development
Network of Pennsylvania
(WEDnetPA), 55–60
Workforce Investment Act (WIA), 53, 82,
86, 136
Workforce Investment Boards (WIBs)
Atlantic Cape May, 51, 52, 53
Kentucky, 84, 85, 87, 95, 101
local, Brownfields Worker Training
Grants and, 118–119
Pennsylvania, 58
Providence/Cranston, RI, 122
Workforce Solutions of
Providence/Cranston, 122
WorkKeys, Owensboro Community and
Technical College, KY, 99, 100, 103
Workplace, Inc., The (CN), 118
Workplace Learning Project, CO, 161–
162
Workplace Learning Resource Center,
WEDnetPA's, 57–58
World-Class Training Center, Tri-County
Technical College, Pendleton, SC,
173–175

ABOUT THE CONTRIBUTORS

Keith Bird was appointed chancellor of the Kentucky Community and Technical College System in February 1999. He previously served as president of Central Carolina Technical College and New Hampshire Regional Community Technical College at Claremont and Nashua.

John F. Blasdell is assistant director of continuing education on the Dubois campus of Penn State University.

Jana Bowers is the director of skills development and training for Northeast Texas Community College, where she has worked for 5 years.

Robert Bowman is executive director and chief executive officer of the New Jersey Consortium for Workforce and Economic Development.

Michael J. Brna is the director of workforce development for the California University of Pennsylvania.

Meghann Cotter writes for *Knight Ridder Tribune Business News.*

Fran Daniel writes for *Knight Ridder Tribune Business News.*

Don C. Garrison has been president of the Tri-County Technical College, Pendleton, South Carolina, since 1971, after previously serving for 6 years as executive vice president of the Greenville, South Carolina, Technical College.

Note. Biographical information for the authors of previously published material may have changed since the date of original publication.

Patrick E. Gerity was named vice president of continuing education, workforce and community development at Westmoreland County Community College in January 2006. He has three degrees from The Pennsylvania State University, including a PhD in workforce education and development with a special emphasis in training and organization development. Gerity has developed, implemented, directed, and evaluated workforce, economic, and community development initiatives at Westmoreland County Community College, Community College of Allegheny County, Slippery Rock University of Pennsylvania, and the Pennsylvania State System of Higher Education. At the State System, Gerity facilitated the design and implementation of a $9 million grant to create the Workforce and Economic Development Network of Pennsylvania (WEDnet PA). He has created, marketed, implemented, and administered customized training courses for over 200 Pittsburgh area businesses and industries and is responsible for acquiring over $10 million in Customized Job Training grants for companies to promote economic development in southwestern Pennsylvania. He is currently a member of the National Council for Workforce Education, University Continuing Education Association, National Council for Continuing Education and Training, American Society of Training and Development, and the Pennsylvania Association for Continuing Education. He has been a presenter at numerous regional, state, and national conferences on workforce development and is AACC's Community College Workforce Development State Liaison for Pennsylvania.

Marilyn Gilroy writes for *The Hispanic Outlook in Higher Education.*

Cecile S. Holmes is an assistant professor in the College of Journalism and Mass Communications at the University of South Carolina.

Joe Iannarelli writes for *Business First.*

James Jacobs is associate vice president of Macomb Community College, Michigan, where he also has served as professor of economics, director of policy research, and director of the center for community studies.

Anne C. Lewis, one of the country's most respected writers on education policy, works in the Washington, DC, area.

Edward McDonnell is vice president and dean, Camden County College.

Mark Mervos is director at the Center for Professional Development at the Community College of Allegheny County, Pittsburgh. He has held various leadership positions at the college, as well as at Ford Motor Company and Pan American Insurance. Community and adult education have been his focus the last 27 years, with emphasis the most recent 10 years on workforce development. His client base ranges from Fortune 500 companies to start ups. He holds a master's degree in higher education from Indiana University of Pennsylvania and a BA in economics from the University of Pittsburgh.

Larry Michael is the executive director for workforce and economic development for Pennsylvania College of Technology. His organization represents a staff of 33 professionals that provide noncredit training, consulting, and certification and testing services to business and industry by coordinating programming with Penn College's 100 majors and 500 faculty.

Valerie Miller writes for the *Las Vegas Business Press.*

Lawrence Nespoli is president of the New Jersey Council of County Colleges.

Patricia A. Owens is dean of continuing education and resource development and executive director of the Atlantic Cape Community College Foundation.

Valerie J. Palamountain works at Piedmont Virginia Community College.

Bob Phillips is at Dyersburg State Community College.

John D. Piccolo is a director of continuing education on the Dubois campus of Penn State University.

Dan Radakovich is vice president for academic affairs at Johnson County Community College, Overland Park, Kansas. He is a former college president and city councilman and has served on various chamber of commerce economic development groups in Wyoming, California, and Kansas.

Jim L. Raughton is vice president for external affairs for Colorado Community College and Occupational Education System in Denver.

William J. Rothwell is a professor of workforce education and development in the Department of Learning and Performance Systems in the College of Education on the University Park campus of Pennsylvania State University. He leads a graduate emphasis in workplace learning and performance. He is also president of Rothwell & Associates, Inc. (www.rothwell-associates.com), a private consulting firm with over 32 multinational corporations on its client list, which specializes in offering services in human resource management, training, and organizational development. He was previously assistant vice president and management development director for the Franklin Life Insurance Company and training director for the

Illinois Office of Auditor General. He has worked full-time in human resource management and employee training and development from 1979 to the present, combining real-world experience with academic and consulting experience. Rothwell has many publications to his credit. Among the most recent are *Instructor Excellence: Mastering the Delivery of Training, 2nd ed.; What CEOs Expect from Corporate Training* (Korean translation); *Competency-Based Human Resource Management* (Chinese translation); *Next Generation Management Development: The Complete Guide and Resource;* and *Handbook of Training Technology: An Introductory Guide to Facilitating Learning with Technology—From Planning Through Evaluation.*

Kent Scheffel is associate vice president of community education and media services, Lewis and Clark Community College.

John J. Sygielski is president of Lord Fairfax Community College. He is a member of AACC's Commission on Economic and Workforce Development. Formerly, he was vice chancellor of workforce and community development services, Virginia Community College System.

Michael Taggart has served as director of workforce development for the Ohio Board of Regents since 1995. A primary responsibility has been providing leadership for the EnterpriseOhio Network, a statewide alliance of 53 two-year campuses that work collaboratively to provide workforce development services to Ohio employers. Before joining the Board of Regents staff, he served as executive director of the Unified Technologies Center of Cuyahoga Community College in Cleveland and as director of the Private Industry Council of Cleveland. He holds an MBA from Baldwin Wallace College and a master's degree in social service administration form Case Western Reserve University.

Tom Venditti currently serves as the statewide director for the Workforce and Economic Development Network of Pennsylvania (WEDnetPA), a statewide collaboration of 33 colleges, universities, and technology centers that administers over $18 million for employee training to over 2,000 companies and 100,000 employees annually through Pennsylvania's Guaranteed Free Training program.

Larry Warford is project director for the College and Career Transitions Initiative, a cooperative agreement between the U.S. Department of Education, Office of Adult and Vocational Education, and the League for Innovation in the Community College. Previously, Warford served as the community college liaison for America's Career Kit in the U.S. Department of Labor. During his more than 30 years of community college leadership, Warford also helped establish Iowa Central Community College, served as vice president for instruction and vice president for community and economic development at Lane Community College, and was a consultant for AACC. Nationally recognized for his research and leadership in workforce training and lifelong learning, Warford makes presentations at national conferences and meetings and has written about comprehensive workforce training, the need for policy change to provide lifelong learning to have a competitive workforce, and other subjects of interest to community college leaders. The results of his national study on state funding for noncredit programs were published in several journals; his research on contract training led to the creation of the national customized training network for community colleges in the League for Innovation in the Community College, as well as the League's national workforce initiative. The League honored him in 1996 for his outstanding leadership in workforce development in the community college. Warford is a past president of NCCET and received that organization's Exemplary Service Award. He has also served on AACC's Workforce and Economic Development Commission and on the Advisory Committee for the Career and Technical Education dissemination project operated by the Ohio State University and the University of Illinois. Warford has a PhD in higher education administration from the University of Oregon and a master's and bachelor's degrees in business and education from the University of Northern Iowa.

Susan J. Wells is a business journalist based in the Washington, DC, area.

Nancy Wong was a copy editor for *Workforce Management* at the time that her original article, reprinted in this volume, was published.

Trenton Wright is coordinator of institutional advancement, Middlesex Community College, Connecticut.